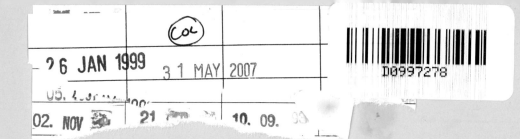

EAST ANGLIA RAILWAYS
Remembered

Leslie Oppitz

COUNTRYSIDE BOOKS
NEWBURY, BERKSHIRE

First Published 1989
© Leslie Oppitz 1989

COUNTRYSIDE BOOKS
3 CATHERINE ROAD
NEWBURY, BERKSHIRE

ISBN 1 85306 040 2

Produced through MRM Associates, Reading
Typeset by Acorn Bookwork, Salisbury
Printed in England

CONTENTS

The following abbreviations are used on numerous occasions in this book:

CVRPS	Colne Valley Railway Preservation Society
ECR	Eastern Counties Railway
ESR	East Suffolk Railway
EUR	Eastern Union Railway
GER	Great Eastern Railway
GNR	Great Northern Railway
GN&GE	Great Northern & Great Eastern Joint Railway
GWR	Great Western Railway
K&T	Kelvedon, Tiptree & Tollesbury Pier Light Railway
M&GN	Midland & Great Northern Joint Committee
MR	Midland Railway
MSLR	Mid-Suffolk Light Railway
MT&W	Mistley, Thorpe & Walton Railway
N&ER	Northern & Eastern Railway
NNR	North Norfolk Railway
T&W	Thetford & Watton Railway
THR	Tendring Hundred Railway
W&B	Wivenhoe & Brightlingsea Railway
W&WLR	Wells & Walsingham Light Railway
WVR	Waveney Valley Railway

BIBLIOGRAPHY

In compiling East Anglia Railways Remembered, I have referred to numerous sources which include the following and which can be recommended for further reading:

Author	Title	Publisher
Cecil J Allen	The Great Eastern Railway	Ian Allan Ltd
R S Joby	Forgotten Railways – East Anglia	David & Charles
D I Gordon	A Regional History of the Railways of Great Britain – Volume 5 The Eastern Counties	David & Charles
Geoffrey Body	Railways of the Eastern Region Volume 1: Southern Operating Area	Book Club Associates by arrangement with Patrick Stephens Ltd
Hugh Moffat	East Anglia's First Railways	Terence Dalton
B D J Walsh	The Stour Valley Railway	Connor & Butler on behalf of the East Anglian Railway Museum
Michael Young	Colne Valley Album	Apex Publications, Cambridge
N J Stapleton	The Kelvedon and Tollesbury Light Railway	Forge Books and Stour Valley Railway Preservation Society
N A Comfort	The Mid-Suffolk Light Railway	Oakwood Press
John M Cooper	The East Suffolk Railway	Oakwood Press
P Paye	The Ely & St Ives Railway	Oakwood Press
C M Wright	The East Anglian Railway Museum	Stour Valley Railway Preservation Society
Keith Philbrick	Wells & Walsingham Light Railway	The Wells & Walsingham Light Railway
Gordon Perry and Michael Park	A Visitor's Guide to the North Norfolk Railway	North Norfolk Railway, Sheringham
John Rhodes	The Midland & Great Northern Joint Railway	Ian Allan Ltd
Edwin Course	Railways Then and Now	B T Batsford Ltd
A Barrett Jenkins	Memories of the Southwold Railway	L & S Rexon Southwold
A T Wallis	Colne Valley Railway Guide and Stock Book	Colne Valley Railway Preservation Society Limited
H I Quayle and Stanley C Jenkins	Branch Lines into the Eighties	David & Charles

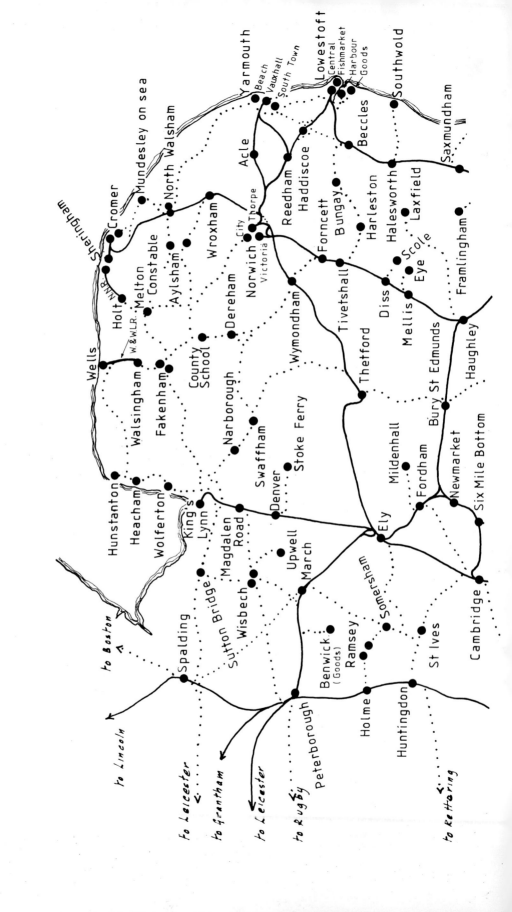

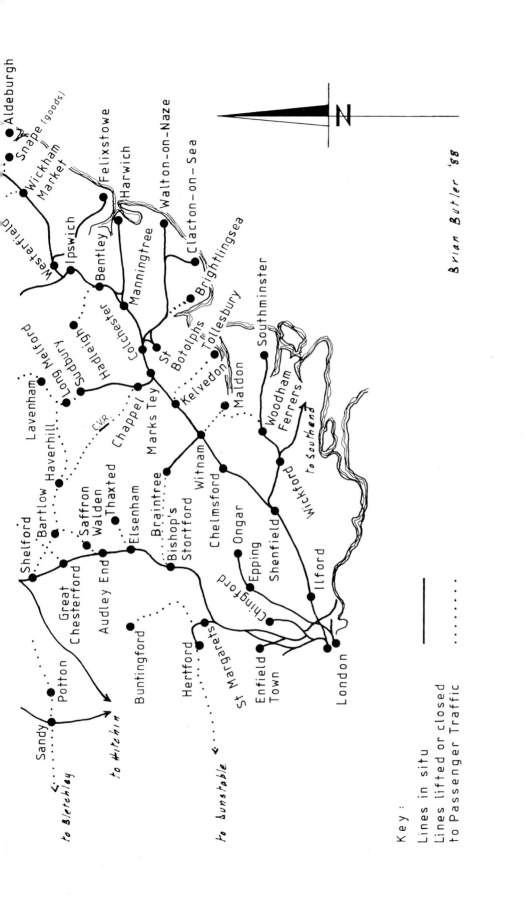

Brian Butler '88

Key:

Lines in situ ────────

Lines lifted or closed
to Passenger Traffic ·········

ACKNOWLEDGEMENTS

Acknowledgements are due to the many libraries and record offices throughout East Anglia who have delved into records and to J L Smith of *Lens of Sutton*, John H Meredith and D Thompson for their help in the supply of many early pictures.

Thanks also go to the following who generously contributed with information: Mr D P Madden, General Manager of The North Norfolk Railway, Chris Johnson of the East Anglian Railway Museum, Lt Cmdr R W Francis of the Wells & Walsingham Light Railway, Alan Bloom of the Bressingham Live Steam Museum, the Colne Valley Railway, Roger Hedley-Walker of Wolferton Station Museum, John Watling of the GER Society and J M C Bunn of the Midland & Great Northern Joint Railway Society. In addition thanks go to Malcolm Cook and H C Howe of the Fakenham & Dereham Railway Society (Wensum Valley Railway) and to Broadland District Council, Norwich, regarding the proposed Bure Valley Railway from Aylsham to Wroxham.

Personal thanks go to the following for their help: Mrs Gloria Abbott of Bury St Edmunds, Desmond Adams, Vernon Deadman, John Hadley of Huntingdon, 'Bob' Jenkins of Fransham, David Jenkins, Nigel Oppitz and B D J Walsh, author of *The Stour Valley Railway*. Finally thanks to Brian Butler for preparing the maps and, as ever, my wife Joan for her patience and assistance.

INTRODUCTION

An almost intact yet deserted station building stands at right angles to a minor road just over a mile from the Norfolk village of East Rudham. Peering into the waiting room from the platform it is possible to see a mirror still hanging on the wall and, in the once busy ticket office next door, book racks stand empty. A buddleia tree almost hides a deserted cycle rack and, not far away, there is an overgrown and rusting 'gents'! Tacked onto the nearby level-crossing gate a notice reads, 'For Sale by Auction'.

The above scene typifies many which can be found today throughout East Anglia. Old station buildings, engine sheds, road bridges or overgrown trackbeds all go to make up what was once a vast network of railways when steam trains made their way across open stretches of countryside, linking remote villages and towns.

First ideas for railways in East Anglia included a proposal in 1836 for a line to be built from London to York via Dunmow, Saffron Walden and Cambridge. Yet of the various plans submitted, those which gained approval were a Northern & Eastern Railway (N&ER) line from Islington to Cambridge and, at the same time, an Eastern Counties Railway (ECR) project to build from Shoreditch to Yarmouth. It was this latter company that was later to overcome many of its rivals and form the eventual basis of the Great Eastern Railway (GER).

Although the N&ER and ECR were both incorporated in 1836, progress was slow. First activity on ECR tracks came on June 18th 1839 when two trains, each with a locomotive fore and aft, proceeded parallel to each other along the 5 foot gauge double track from a temporary terminus at Mile End to another temporary structure at Romford. Guns were fired in salute and guests were entertained by the band of the Coldstream Guards.

Yet the ECR soon experienced financial problems and it was another year before Brentwood was reached. There were disputes with landowners and, to make matters worse, shareholders in Norfolk and Suffolk began proceedings to acquire the land so that construction at their end of the line could commence. By 1843, seven years after the two companies had been incorporated, the N&ER had only reached as far as Bishop's Stortford and the ECR had reached Colchester.

In 1844 there were two important events. Firstly, the ECR took over the working of the N&ER although the latter remained a separate company for many years. Secondly, both companies (showing more foresight than the GWR) changed their gauge from 5 foot to 4 foot 8½ inches conforming to the many other railways of the day.

Meantime, the Norfolk shareholders, frustrated at the ECR's slow progress, promoted their own Yarmouth & Norwich company to build a line which opened on May 1st 1844. In order to improve communication with London, a further company, the Norwich & Brandon Railway, was formed. Both this company and the Yarmouth & Norwich were later to be united as the Norfolk Railway. Eventually on July 30th 1845, Norwich was reached from London via Cambridge when the Norfolk Railway met the ECR's route from London at Brandon.

Further lines followed. The Eastern Union Railway (EUR), also frustrated with the ECR's lack of progress, was formed, with trains soon to reach Norwich via Ipswich but the EUR succumbed to the ECR in 1854. From 1859 the East Suffolk Railway provided a direct link between Ipswich and the towns of Lowestoft and Yarmouth, yet even this was operated by the ECR from the day it opened.

A large number of East Anglia's branch lines came about through the ECR's failure to build new lines. The company gained a reputation for poor services and bad time-keeping and it had no money for expansion. Because of this, many districts requiring railway access had to promote their own lines or come to terms with the ECR. On August 1st 1862, the ECR was incorporated into the GER.

Another major route stretching across much of the Fens and Norfolk was that of the Midland & Great Northern Joint Committee (M&GN). These lines had been formed out of a number of independent companies which eventually became the M&GN on July 1st 1893.

The majority of East Anglia's railways were built in the second half of the 19th century. In numerous instances passenger traffic remained light throughout, although goods traffic provided an essential service to the many agricultural areas. Some lines suffered an early demise during the period around 1930 simply because they had become uneconomic. Road transport was fast competing and, when the Beeching cuts of the early 1960s came, there were many more closures.

This book intends to examine not only the lives of these lines, their decline and closure but also covers the many preservation societies that are today dedicated to keep the past alive. Apart from providing the reader with a means to explore the many 'lost' stations and trackbeds that have survived, the book includes details of the numerous societies, both active at the present time and those anticipated in the future.

Chapter 1

GREAT EASTERN LINES FROM KING'S LYNN

King's Lynn to Hunstanton

A steam train arrives at Wolferton station pulling up with the main doorway of the Royal Saloon exactly opposite the double doors to the station's main hallway. A visiting King and Queen alight to be greeted by King Edward VII and Queen Alexandra. The gentlemen make for King Edward's room for a drink and a smoke and the ladies go to the larger and lighter room of Queen Alexandra to take tea.

With the Royals out of the way, the hard work begins. The accompanying servants unload the baggage and set off on the walk of over two miles to Sandringham House. The mountains of trunks and cases are then loaded onto carts by further servants and hauled up the hill to Sandringham where the bags are taken to the appropriate rooms. There the proper attire is laid out for the forthcoming formal reception.

When completed, word passes back to Wolferton station where the Royals are still entertaining their guests. Often an inspection of the troops paraded in the station drive followed, after which the Royal party proceed by carriage to Sandringham.

The above scene could be witnessed many times at Wolferton station on the line from King's Lynn to Hunstanton, with the station's greatest period undoubtedly in the early 1900s during the reign of King Edward VII. Even so, between 1884 and 1911, no fewer than 645 Royal Trains steamed into or out of this little station.

Wolferton station on the King's Lynn to Hunstanton line photographed in September 1988. Once the haunt of Royalty, the station became a railway museum in April 1977, eight years after the line had closed to passenger traffic. (Author)

The King's Lynn to Hunstanton line closed on May 3rd 1969 yet Wolferton station survived – thanks only to the efforts of the Hedley-Walker family. The fine building has become a museum containing many fascinating Royal and railway *objects d'art* and memorabilia. Well worth a visit, it can be found just off the A149 and is open to visitors from April to September inclusive plus Bank Holidays.

Trains first reached King's Lynn in 1846 and the town had not particularly welcomed them. The port authorities claimed that their trade would decline instead of expand and, when a through line to London became available, their deliberations proved correct with the majority of goods carried direct to the capital by rail. The line from King's Lynn to Hunstanton opened on October 3rd 1862 and a branch from Heacham to Wells followed on August 17th 1866. The lines were initially assured of success for this was a time when holiday makers were coming to the Norfolk coast in large numbers. Hunstanton was promoted as a new resort and the many visitors by rail ensured that the line worked at a profit.

Heacham/Wells/Fakenham

Heacham Junction, about a mile west of the village, was the usual place to change trains for Wells although some specials went straight through. Today the remains of the station can still be found on a camp site next to 'The West Norfolk' public house. Some 200 yards to the north an old signal box has just about survived the years. At the pub, the chalked menu on the board above the bar nostalgically carried the message 'Menu approved by BR'!

Hunstanton station long ago surrendered to the motor age, being today the resort's large car park. However, following the abandoned line through to Wells proved interesting. Sedgeford station building remains as a private house complete with its station sign and GER notices. On the level-crossing gate a notice read 'Failure to shut the gate – fine 40/-'. Docking and Stanhoe were also preserved as private dwellings but Burnham Market was now part of Burnham Motor Garage. At Wells, correctly known as Wells-next-the-Sea, the station building has become Burnham Potteries. The owner bemoaned that the only relic of the past that remained was the Ladies Room sign. Not far from Wells station just off the A149 can be found the Wells & Walsingham Light Railway which opened in 1982 along a stretch of ten and a quarter inch gauge track (see chapter 3).

The Wells & Fakenham Railway opened on December 1st 1857. When it became part of the GER in 1862 it assumed greater importance becoming part of a north–south line carrying food to London's increasing markets. The intermediate town of Walsingham had been for many centuries one of England's major religious pilgrimage centres attracting Royalty and commoners alike. When the railway became available, many thousands would frequently alight from specials on occasions of major festivals to form processions to either the Anglican or Roman Catholic shrine in the different parts of the town. Often there were 'Roman Catholic Specials' which would halt about a mile short of the station nearer the shrine.

The line closed to passengers on October 5th 1954, surviving for goods traffic only until the end of the month. It was perhaps appropriate that Walsingham station should become a Russian Orthodox Monastery. The station building acquired golden domes with services held in the old booking hall.

Not far from The West Norfolk *public house at Heacham can be found an old signal box that once stood where a branch line to Wells left the Hunstanton line. Nearby once stood Heacham station, now part of a camp site. (Author)*

King's Lynn to Dereham

The line from King's Lynn to Dereham opened in various stages from 1846 to 1848. The Lynn & Dereham Railway became part of the East Anglian Railway in 1847 and, like the Wells & Fakenham Railway, was incorporated into the GER in 1862. The cost to build the line had been high due to inflated land prices, a much criticised policy of bulk buying iron when prices were high and, not least, a difficult chalk cutting at Swaffham.

Even though the promoters had great hopes for the line, the single track initially carried only three or four trains daily, rising to nine early this century. In September 1955 diesel multiple-units were introduced but, despite such economies, the line closed completely on September 9th 1968 except for a short stretch for freight from King's Lynn to Middleton.

Stations worth visiting along the line today include Swaffham, Dunham and Fransham. Swaffham has become a community centre (chapter 6) and at Dunham the station building has become part of a museum which includes stationary engines, pumps and 'various bygones'. The goods shed is used by a company making furniture.

At Fransham, although a private residence, the garden proved a railway historian's delight. Not only did the station building and platform still exist, but rolling stock standing on short sections of track included an industrial locomotive, an old coach and 0-6-0 steam locomotive.

The industrial locomotive is a preserved Ruston & Hornby 88DS diesel shunter which was first used by a steel works at Wednesbury in June 1956. Passenger coach no 1235, however,

Wells-next-the-Sea station closed on October 31st 1964. The station building in September 1988 had become Burnham Potteries and the owner bemoaned that all that remained of the past was a Ladies Room sign! (Lens of Sutton)

At Fransham on the King's Lynn to Dereham line, not only has the station building survived as a private residence but rolling stock includes a Ruston & Hornby 88DS diesel shunter and a five compartment 4 wheel suburban coach built at Stratford in 1891. (Author)

started life as a 5 compartment 4 wheel suburban carriage built at Stratford Works in December 1891. In 1902 it was widened from 8 feet to 9 feet wide to correspond with the new 6-a-side suburban stock that had been introduced in 1899. The coach was withdrawn in July 1926, still in suburban use.

The Hudswell Clarke 0-6-0 locomotive, works no 1208, dates back to 1916 when it was one of three identical locomotives built for the Ministry of Munitions, each at a cost of £1545! The engine is unusual in having outside cylinders and outside valve gear. In the past users have included the Nidd Valley Railway (Yorkshire), McAlpines and the RAF at Swinnerton. 'Bob' Jenkins at Fransham rescued it from a scrapyard in July 1988 and, with his wife's help, hopes to restore the locomotive to working condition.

Magdalen Road to Wisbech

The line from Magdalen Road to Wisbech was originally part of the East Anglian Railway system, another to be incorporated into the GER in 1862. Magdalen Road, known as Watlington until 1875, became a junction in 1848 when a branch to Wisbech was completed. Intermediate stations were Middle Drove, Smeeth Road and Emneth. The line lasted until 1964 for goods and was closed to passengers on September 9th 1968. Magdalen Road station on the main Ely to King's Lynn also closed on September 9th 1968 but re-opened May 5th 1975 following local efforts to encourage the use of trains.

Magdalen Road station still boasts a signal box but the level crossing has become automatic. The station buildings however were fenced off from the platform in common with the current BR policy to lease out station buildings wherever possible.

Wisbech station (spelled Wisbeach until May 1877) became Wisbech East in September 1948. The town once boasted two separate stations and two harbour branches (M&GN and GER)

Passenger traffic along the branch line from Denver to Stoke Ferry which opened in August 1882 was poor throughout. Despite economies, passenger traffic came to an end in September 1930 although goods survived until April 1965. The terminus and goods buildings are seen here at the turn of the century. (Lens of Sutton)

and a standard-gauge tramway to Upwell (see chapter 15) but these were not to last. The M&GN line closed in 1959 and the Harbour North branch closed in 1965. Next came the Harbour East branch which, together with the Wisbech & Upwell Tramway, closed the following year.

When the GER station closed in 1968, a freight only line remained in existence from Whitemoor junction (north of March) to Wisbech goods yard for the conveyance of Spillers pet food, Metal Box products plus coal traffic. Apart from this occasional freight traffic, Wisbech has little today to remind its inhabitants of its previous railway connections. Wisbech (East) station building has survived, currently serving as a centre for mentally-handicapped children.

Denver to Stoke Ferry

There were no serious difficulties during construction of the branch to Stoke Ferry except where the ground was found to be very boggy. Numerous culverts were necessary and in one instance time was lost filling in a pond. The construction of Stoke Ferry station provided the greatest obstacle because of marshland. It proved necessary to remove the top-soil to a depth of twelve feet and then build brick arches to support the building and platform.

Services began on August 1st 1882 with a service of six trains daily between Stoke Ferry and Downham Market with some going on to King's Lynn. In 1905 a private standard-gauge railway opened, leaving the branch at the intermediate station of Abbey & West Dereham to reach the estate of A J Keeble and also assist in Fenland drainage.

Passenger traffic to Stoke Ferry was poor and economies became necessary. Ticket offices along the branch were closed and conductor–guard working was introduced. Freight traffic helped

to keep the line busy and the building of a sugar beet factory at Wissington in 1925 did much to increase the branch's status.

By the middle 1920s bus competition was taking what little passenger traffic remained. It came as no surprise when the branch closed to passengers on September 22nd 1930 although freight traffic was to continue for a number of years. In 1941 the Ministry of Agriculture took over the Wissington lines followed by purchase six years later. In 1957 all the tracks south of the sugar factory were closed and on April 19th 1965 the line beyond Abbey & West Dereham closed except for use as a siding. All that remained was the freight traffic between Denver and the Wissington factory which was to survive some years further.

When visiting Stoke Ferry in September 1988, the author found the station building and goods shed still in existence but the water tower, the crane and the signal box had gone. The station had become a private residence and the goods shed was used by timber merchants. In the station approach there was a 'mobile' doctor's surgery.

While walking the area, there had been a shout across the yard from 78-year old 'Ernie' Pedditt, Leading Porter at Stoke Ferry from 1942 to 1965. He had called, 'If you're here to catch a train, the last one went nearly 60 years ago . . .'

The site of Stoke Ferry station in September 1988. The station building is a private residence, the goods yard is used by a timber merchant and a 'mobile' doctor's surgery is adjacent to the drive. (Author)

Chapter 2

MIDLAND & GREAT NORTHERN JOINT LINES IN NORFOLK AND THE FENS

By the time the Eastern Counties Railway (ECR) reached King's Lynn in 1848 and Wells-next-the Sea in 1849, the company was in truculent mood. It claimed that its network left 'not a single opening for any rival line'. However, circumstances were to prove otherwise, although it took many years for the rival Midland & Great Northern Joint Railway (M&GN) to make its presence felt.

Yet not all went well for the Eastern Counties Railway. In 1860 it was claimed that its trains were no longer punctual, its fares and freight rates were excessive and accidents were far too frequent. The company's finances worsened and on August 7th 1862, the ECR became part of the newly-formed Great Eastern Railway. Meanwhile rivalry continued with the Midland Railway (MR) and the Great Northern Railway (GNR) joining forces to gain access to the east coast.

The first foothold in East Anglia came in November 1858 when the Norwich & Spalding Railway Company completed eight miles of track from Spalding to Holbeach. Sutton Bridge was reached nearly four years later in July 1862. Earlier, on August 6th 1861, an Act had been approved granting the Lynn & Sutton Bridge Railway powers to build a line from Sutton Bridge to a junction with the ECR Ely–King's Lynn line near South Lynn. Further Acts followed. In 1862 came agreement to build from Spalding to

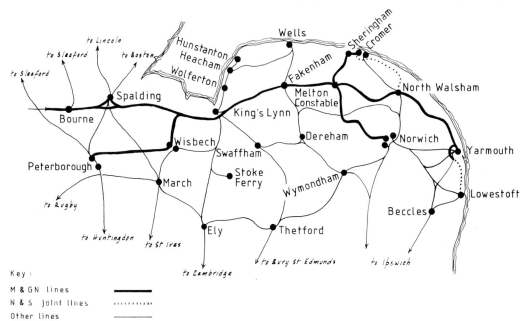

Key:

M & GN lines

N & S Joint lines

Other lines

Bourne and in July 1866 the three companies amalgamated to form the Midland & Eastern Railway.

Further gains followed in East Norfolk when in January 1883 the Lynn & Fakenham Railway, the Yarmouth & North Norfolk and the Yarmouth Union amalgamated to form the Eastern & Midlands Railway. The amalgamation also included the Peterborough, Wisbech & Sutton Bridge Railway which, until that time, had remained independent. In July 1883 the Eastern & Midlands Railway went on to absorb the Midland & Eastern Railway.

The Midland Railway (MR) and the GNR had throughout maintained strong interests in these various companies (there were even suggestions of financial backing) and it was a logical progression when on July 1st 1893, the Midland & Great Northern Joint Railway (M&GN) was formed which at the same time took over the Eastern & Midlands. A company crest, adapted from that of the Eastern & Midlands Railway, incorporated the coats of arms of the principal cities served, Peterborough, Norwich, King's Lynn and Yarmouth.

Moulton station between Spalding and Sutton Bridge closed to passengers in March 1959. Today the waiting room on the up line has become 'The Travellers' Rest', housing a small bar. Station House opposite provides Bed & Breakfast accommodation. (Author)

Lines from Sutton Bridge

A line from Spalding to Sutton Bridge opened on July 3rd 1862 with the further section to South Lynn following nearly three years later on March 1st 1865. On August 1st 1866 a line opened westwards from Spalding to Bourne and, later in 1893, trains reached Little Bytham Junction, later to be officially described as the M&GN system's furthest westerly point.

Travelling by car from Spalding towards South Lynn, Weston

A steam locomotive, probably a 4-4-0 Beyer Peacock, at Sutton Bridge c1910. The station opened in July 1862 serving lines westwards beyond Spalding. By 1865 trains reached South Lynn and in the following year a line reached Peterborough via Wisbech. (Lens of Sutton)

station was not easy to find. The station building remained as a private dwelling although considerably altered. It was so isolated that it was difficult to imagine it could ever have been much used, being some 1½ miles from Weston itself.

Moulton station closed to passengers on March 2nd 1959 and to goods traffic on June 15th 1964. Since that time the property has had a varied life. It was bought in 1969 from BR by a potato merchant but the large goods shed suffered a serious fire in 1974 when struck by lightning after which time the station building remained empty for a time. In 1978 the Smith family moved in and slowly a remarkable transformation took place.

After many years of hard work, Chris and Judith Smith turned 'Station House' into a fine family home. Yet there are still many reminders from the railway age. Much of the up platform has gone but the old waiting room remains – perfectly preserved. Now called 'The Travellers' Rest', it houses a small bar which might well have been appreciated in earlier times. The Smith family also provide a bed & breakfast service and any male visitor fortunate enough to enjoy a meal in the fine dining room may well care to recall that he is sitting in what was once the Ladies Waiting Room!

The road swing bridge at Cross Keys across the river Nene is worth a visit. When the Lynn & Sutton Bridge Railway built eastwards from Sutton Bridge, the existing 1850 cast and wrought iron bridge designed by Robert Stephenson shared road and rail traffic, the latter crossing the river by a single track. Towards the end of the century the bridge proved inadequate and a new structure was built in 1897 slightly to the south, the change of location being the reason for the subsequent sharp curve out of Sutton Bridge station. The new bridge was operated by hydraulic

Before closure of the M&GN South Lynn/ Spalding line in the 1960s, Cross Keys bridge which spans the river Nene east of Sutton Bridge station carried a rail and road section. The bridge, seen here in September 1988, was built in 1897 since the previous structure had proved inadequate. (Author)

Massingham station, between King's Lynn and Fakenham, closed to passengers in March 1959 but it has been delightfully preserved as a private dwelling. Relics to be found include a signal box built earlier this century, an old lamp room and a plate-layers' hut. (Author)

power and the cost of building, £80,000, was borne by the M&GN. When the railways closed in the 1960s, the rail trackbed was turned into a road surface, now carrying westbound traffic.

A line southwards from Sutton Bridge via Wisbech (described as Wisbeach in the Act) to Peterborough opened to passengers on August 1st 1866. M&GN trains left the Midland main line just north of Peterborough North station crossing the main lines by Rhubarb Bridge, so called because when the embankments were built up from nearby farms, rhubarb roots continued to flourish in the earth for many years. Apart for providing a useful route for holiday makers making for the east coast each summer, the line also became busy with the carriage of fruit and agricultural products.

When visited in September 1988, East Rudham station buildings remained almost intact although somewhat overgrown! The station, between King's Lynn and Fakenham, closed to passengers in 1959. (Author)

The bus shelter on the B1354 at Melton Constable carries reminders of earlier times. Apart from a drawing of a 4-4-2 tank locomotive, it includes two spandrels originally from the railway station. (Author)

By 1900, there were 5,000 acres of fruit, flowers and vegetation within only a few miles of Wisbech. The peak came in the 1930s by which time up to sixty wagons daily were leaving the area for many principal towns throughout the country. Vegetables and soft fruit were seasonal but potatoes were carried the whole year round. Later in the year came sugar beet and, after Christmas, the flower trade provided traffic for several months.

Today, some 30 years after closure of the lines to passengers, numerous intermediate stations can still be found. Many are now private dwellings although Sutton Bridge station site became an industrial area. The Wisbech M&GN station gave way to housing with 'Cricketers' Way' marking the site. South of King's Lynn a loop line had opened in 1885 for goods and 1886 for passengers but when this finally closed in 1968, the only people to benefit were motorists, when a bypass was built on the trackbed.

King's Lynn to Norwich and the Norfolk Coast

The Lynn & Fakenham Railway was agreed per an Act of 1876 between King's Lynn and Fakenham and a further Act of 1880 from Fakenham via Melton Constable to Norwich City. Trains reached Massingham in 1879, Fakenham in 1880 and Melton Constable in 1882. By December 2nd 1882, trains had reached Norwich. Services from Melton Constable to the coast at Cromer followed five years later on June 16th 1887. Initially the GER station at King's Lynn was used, leaving the Hunstanton branch at Gaywood Junction. When the Lynn loop line opened in 1886, the Gaywood section was closed and trains could now travel from stations such as Sutton Bridge to Norfolk without reversal.

At the centre of what was to become the M&GN's eastern section was Melton Constable. The year before the railways came, the parish had a population of 118 but the area developed rapidly after a railway junction had been constructed and a railway works established. The once quiet locality soon echoed to the sound of freight trains being shunted or locomotives being serviced in a running shed. To encourage labour in such an isolated place, houses were built and the railway company paid the rents. The first houses constructed in Melton Street and Astley Terrace, although of poor quality, were built for £150 each!

The works buildings were constructed with brick and iron and made to last, being still in existence to this day. A gasworks, sewage works and a water tower were also provided. The water tower can be found above the factory area and closer inspection shows where shrapnel holes from Second World War bombs have been success-fully 'patched up' following a German air raid. Another reminder of earlier times is the bus shelter near a road junction on the B1354. In addition to a town sign on the side wall which includes a drawing of a tank locomotive, the shelter also incorporates two

Trains reached Norwich City station, seen here in June 1955, from Melton Constable in 1882. After closure to passengers in March 1959 and to goods traffic in February 1969, the station was demolished to become an industrial site. (D Thompson)

ornamental spandrels which originated from Melton Constable station. Unexpectedly the spandrels carry the initials CNR which stand for the Central Norfolk Railway – a company that never obtained an Act but was promoted to provide a link between Melton Constable and North Walsham. The line was eventually built by the Lynn & Fakenham with the co-operation of the Yarmouth & North Norfolk.

A number of station buildings still exist along the line eastwards from King's Lynn. In September 1988, Hillington station and platform, complete with awning, was up for sale. At Massingham, 'Station House', situated on the side of a hill, was in superb condition. Today a private dwelling, the space between the platforms had been filled in and, not far away, the signal box remained in good condition. The old lamp room, a platelayers' hut, a well house plus pieces of fencing were all among the relics to be seen.

Between Melton Constable and Norwich, Lenwade station building, platform and level crossing remain, the area used by private industry. At Attlebridge, the platform and the level crossing gate still exist but the station building has been demolished to make way for a private house. Drayton station had gone and the area is used industrially but northwards the trackbed has become a footpath. At the terminus, Norwich City has gone and the site has been lost under a road scheme.

At the turn of the century the GER and the M&GN formed joint ventures known as the Norfolk & Suffolk Joint Committee. One such line was from Cromer to North Walsham, which included this resort of Mundesley-on-Sea. The station closed in 1964. (Lens of Sutton)

Northwards from Melton Constable the line between Holt and Sheringham is currently put to good use by the North Norfolk Railway (see chapter 3). In contrast to the original Sheringham station, now the North Norfolk Railway terminus, the BR station across the road seemed little more than an apology. Despite this some twelve DMUs ply daily between Sheringham and Norwich. The line to Cromer (previously Cromer Beach) uses the former M&GN route. Since Cromer is a terminus, a reversal is necessary after which the DMUs use track once worked by the Norfolk & Suffolk Joint Railways Committee – a joint co-operation between

the M&GN and the GER to avoid unnecessary duplication of routes. Subsequently the trains join the former GER line south of Cromer High (closed to passengers in 1954) to reach Norwich. At Cromer station it is possible to see where once extensive sidings existed and the station building still carries the E&MR motif (Eastern & Midlands Railway) in its arched supports.

Cromer High station c1910. It was opened by the East Norfolk Railway (later GER) when a route from Norwich was completed in 1877. The station closed in September 1954 when Cromer Beach (today known merely as Cromer) became the town's only station. (Lens of Sutton)

The most easterly point reached by the M&GN was Yarmouth Beach. The route from Melton Constable via North Walsham was agreed per numerous Acts between 1876 and 1881 and opened in sections over a six year period with completion over the whole route in April 1883. By 1887 King's Lynn services included trains to Cromer, Norwich and Yarmouth and, over further Norfolk & Suffolk Joint Railways Committee tracks, trains to Mundesley and Lowestoft. In July 1906 co-operation between the M&GN and GER went further to provide a London-Sheringham service. A year later the 'Norfolk Coast Express' came into being with sections for Sheringham, Cromer High and Mundesley.

Decline and Closure

After the First World War, competition came from motorbuses and then from the private motor car. In addition many stations were a mile or so from the towns or villages they claimed to serve. Norwich City station was also some way from the city's commercial centre. It was clear that the heyday of railway monopoly was over. Despite economies, passenger and freight traffic continued to decline although the Second World War did provide a substantial reprieve with many aerodromes in the area.

February 28th 1959 was a sad day for M&GN supporters when almost the entire system closed to passenger trains. Many travelled dressed in black, complete with arm bands and top hat. The

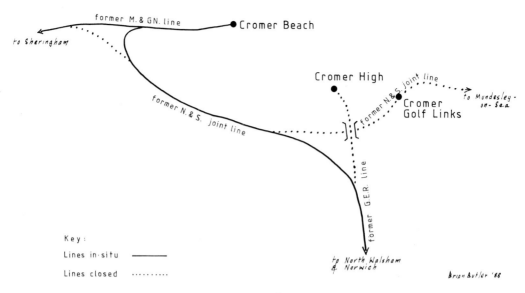

former M. & GN. line

Cromer Beach

to Sheringham

Cromer High

former N. & S. joint line

to Mundesley-on-Sea

Cromer Golf Links

former N. & S. joint line

former G.E.R. line

Key:

Lines in·situ ———

Lines closed ·········

to North Walsham & Norwich

Brian Butler '88

locomotive hauling the last train bound for Melton Constable, 4MT no 43145, was decorated with a laurel wreath on its smoke-box and a slogan, 'Goodbye all: We may not pass this way again' had been written. As the train left the station in a last defiant burst of steam, yards of toilet paper and coloured streamers trailed from its carriage windows.

The line between Sheringham and Melton Constable survived a further five years until closure for passengers came on 4th April 1964. Freight services continued over many lines but these were all destined for eventual failure. The writing on the rear of a brake van on the last diesel-hauled freight train from Sutton Bridge on April 2nd 1965 seemed to sum it all up. It read simply: 'That's yer lot!'

Chapter 3

PRESERVED STEAM IN NORFOLK

Wells & Walsingham Light Railway

When the narrow-gauge railway from Wells to Walsingham opened in 1982 it was an immediate success. Preliminary work to re-open the line had started in 1979, including the obtaining of the necessary Light Railway Order from the Department of Transport.

The promoters of the Wells & Walsingham Light Railway (W&WLR) had a lot of hard work to do. Four miles of 10¼ inch narrow-gauge track needed to be laid, fences and bridges repaired and years of neglect put right. Near Walsingham, a cutting had been filled in with rubbish and had to be dug out again! Even so services began on schedule on April 6th 1982, the day after the Light Railway Order was granted, making it the longest 10¼ inch narrow-gauge railway in the world.

Initially trains comprised an articulated set of four open carriages hauled by an 0-6-0 side tank locomotive named *Pilgrim*, built specially for the line by David King Engineering of North Walsham. *Pilgrim* had two 6 inches by 4 inches cylinders and a working steam pressure of 125 lbs per square inch. For its size it coped well with its four well-filled coaches over the 4 miles to Walsingham which included a climb of 1 in 29 on part of the journey.

Lt. Cmdr. Roy Francis sits at the controls of his unique 2-6-0 + 0-6-2 Garratt steam locomotive 'Norfolk Hero' prior to a regular passenger run along the longest 10¼ inch gauge railway in the world. (Author)

Tracklaying and points installation in progress at the North Norfolk Railway's Holt station at the southern end of the line. This is to be a replica of the original station but at a different site being built just off the A148 King's Lynn to Fakenham road. (Author)

The railway proved not only a strong tourist attraction but also gave a service to people living in the villages along the route because the trains proved to be more regular and frequent than the local bus service. Soon it was found that not all the intending passengers could be carried, particularly during the popular summer months, so a further coach was ordered in 1984 to be delivered the following year. The total seating capacity was now up to 52 per journey but even this soon proved inadequate and it was realised that the potential requirements were beyond *Pilgrim's* capacity.

In July 1985 an 0-6-0 petrol-driven locomotive to be named *Weasel* was purchased from Alan Keef Limited and this provided a short-term solution. At the same time, bearing in mind the fact that people really prefer steam, thought was given by the W&WLR as to how to provide a steam locomotive adequate for the job. Problems with *Pilgrim* had shown that a conventional steam locomotive was not adequate and a totally different approach was needed.

The solution came following consultations with Neil Simkins, a consulting engineer from Ashby-de-la-Zouch, with the result that an unusual and unique design was considered. The idea was to build a Garratt type of locomotive which had twice the power of *Pilgrim*, to be achieved by providing two engine units which would be articulated and have a cradle slung between them carrying the boiler, firebox and cab. The design was agreed and, following a successful share flotation plus a grant from the English Tourist Board, construction began in the autumn of 1985. It was a very proud day for Lt Cmdr Roy Francis, who had pioneered the W&WLR and the many friends of the railway when, on October 18th 1986, the Viscountess Coke of Holkham named the new locomotive *Norfolk Hero*.

Anyone visiting the W&WLR today will see the progress being

made. The railway is open seven days a week from Easter to September with six trains each way daily during peak times. At Wells station, just off the A149 coast road, a shop forms part of a signal box acquired from BR at Swainsthorpe, made redundant through the Norwich 1987 electrification scheme. There are plans to extend as well. There are hopes that perhaps by 1990 trains may be reaching beyond Walsingham to Houghton St Giles, about a mile further on.

The North Norfolk Railway

If perhaps in the past you think you might have recognised Weybourne station in episodes of *Hi-Di-Hi* or *Allo! Allo!* then you would have been right. The station has been the setting for many productions over the years also including a *Miss Marple* feature set in 1949 and, on another occasion, the *Dads' Army* episode of *The Royal Train*. There was even a time when Weybourne was covered with artificial snow to provide a background for the film *Fall of Eagles*.

When the railway between Sheringham and Melton Constable closed at the end of 1964, there were numerous ambitious schemes put forward by the 'M&GN Preservation Society' to save certain of the old lines. The initial ideas proved impractical but the society was eventually able to raise enough money to save the 3 mile section from Weybourne to the station boundary at Sheringham. Unfortunately the paperwork took time and by completion demolition contractors had moved in, removing all the track and sidings at Weybourne and had worked some way towards Sheringham.

In 1967, British Rail abandoned the original Sheringham station

The original Holt station seen here before its final closure in December 1964. The site was later used for the rebuilding of a town bypass. (Lens of Sutton)

in favour of a halt on the other side of the main road. The society immediately took a lease on the building and transferred its activities there. The prospect of operating a preserved railway had now become more practical and to this end a private company, Central Norfolk Enterprises Limited, was formed. Two years later in 1969 it became the North Norfolk Railway Company (NNR) and went public, initially raising £14,000.

During this time volunteers had been relaying the track and sidings ready for the locomotives and rolling stock already purchased. These included two steam locomotives, two Diesel Railbuses and a set of 1924 ex-King's Cross Suburban Quad-art coaches. In 1976 the NNR was granted a Light Railway Order by the Department of the Environment and a regular passenger service between Sheringham and Weybourne was soon to follow.

Since that date steady progress has been made. Thanks to the hard work of many volunteers and additional help given through the Manpower Service Commission schemes, further track has been laid from Weybourne to Kelling Camp Halt (reached in 1983) and Holt. The original 1887 Holt station disappeared with the building of a town bypass many years ago, so the NNR plan a replica just off the A148 King's Lynn-Fakenham road. Fortunately the land is wide enough at the site for this marks an area where a branch line was once planned (but never built) to serve the coastal villages of Salthouse, Cley and Blakeney.

Further work carried out includes the removal and restoration of three signal boxes, the establishment of souvenir shops and catering facilities and the restoration of locomotives – including the popular 0-6-0 ex-GER J15 no 7564. Passenger coaches too form

Weybourne station around the time of closure by British Rail in 1964. Despite the endeavours of the 'M&GN Preservation Society', BR removed all the track and sidings at Weybourne before the society could raise sufficient capital (Lens of Sutton)

an important part of the railway and these include two 'Brighton Belle' cars, one of which has been adapted for use by disabled travellers. Future projects include the completion of Holt station (a share prospectus has been issued), the introduction of signalling at Weybourne so that trains may pass and further on-train catering using a second 'Brighton Belle' car.

Weybourne station, September 1988, now an intermediate station on the North Norfolk Railway line between Sheringham and Holt and preserved in the former M&GN style. The station has been used on numerous occasions in episodes of TV's 'Hi-di-Hi', 'Dad's Army' and many others. (Author)

The author enjoyed a journey on one of the German built ex-BR railbuses. Between Weybourne and Sheringham the railbus passed Deadman's Hill. It is said this got its name because Weybourne's victims of the Great Plague were buried there – at a safe distance from their homes. On entering Sheringham station it was possible to see many of the locomotives, coaches and goods vehicles, forming today's formidable stock list.

On platform 2 could be seen the W H Smith bookstall on long-term loan from the National Railway Museum which had once stood on the concourse of London's Waterloo station. Another exhibit worth seeing was the Gresley buffet car no 51769 originally built by the LNER at York in 1937. This car was in superb condition and a fine example of restoration work masterminded by volunteer Steve Allen.

The North Norfolk Railway, sometimes known as the 'Poppy Line', uses a route which was at one time part of the Midland & Great Northern Joint Railway system. The M&GN, known to many as the 'Joint', was sometimes affectionately called the 'muddle and get nowhere railway'. With its enthusiasm and future prospects, such a description could hardly be given to the North Norfolk Railway.

Bressingham Live Steam Museum
Located on the A1066 Diss–Thetford Road, the Bressingham Live Steam Museum is a haven for locomotive enthusiasts. Yet Bressingham is known not only for its steam museum but also its

An exhibit worth seeing at Sheringham is the Gresley buffet car no 51769 originally built by the LNER at York. The car is in first class condition with restoration having been masterminded by volunteer Steve Allen. (Author)

The W H Smith bookstall at Sheringham is on long-term loan from the National Railway Museum, having stood for many years on the concourse of London's Waterloo station. (Author)

enchanting gardens, an interest started by owner Alan Bloom with his young family in 1946 when he purchased Bressingham Hall Farm to run a nursery business. At first not all went well but slowly their efforts won through.

The first interest in steam came in 1961 when Alan Bloom, already interested in restoring an old 1912 Burrell traction engine, purchased another Burrell which he named *Bertha*. This was soon put to steam and it was immediately noticeable that visitors were taking more than a passing interest. By the end of the year eight engines stood in the yard, most of them derelict and awaiting restoration.

By 1965 the enthusiasm spread to railway locomotives when a 750 yard 9½ inch narrow-gauge track became operational carrying passengers alongside the garden. Half a mile of 2 foot gauge track followed, the rolling stock purchased from a slate quarry in North Wales where steam had given way to diesel lorries. The trains, hauled initially by a little 0-4-0 Hunslet named *George Sholto* were so well patronised that track extensions were soon necessary.

The idea of a steam museum to house standard gauge locomotives came in 1967 soon after the Beeching cuts had taken full effect. At first, locomotives offered were out of reach financially but when British Rail later suggested that engines could be sent out on permanent loan to private organisations or museums, then Alan Bloom acted. During the winter of 1967/8 a shed covering 12,500 square feet was erected and when completed was passed as suitable. The first locomotive to arrive was *William Francis*, the last remaining 0-4-0 + 0-4-0T Beyer-Peacock Garratt in Britain, a unique articulated engine, similar in design to that used on the narrow-gauge Wells & Walsingham Railway. Another destined for Bressingham was *Thundersley*, a 4-4-2 tank built in 1909 for the London, Tilbury & Southend Railway, which was housed at Attleborough for several weeks whilst restored by members of the Norfolk Railway Society.

When the BR Standard Class 7 Pacific locomotive, no 70013, *Oliver Cromwell*, arrived in August 1968 there was great excitement. This engine had been selected to head the last steam-hauled train by British Rail and the trip had been made from Liverpool to Carlisle. From Carlisle it steamed through the night across country to Norwich from where it later travelled to Diss station to be loaded for road transport. At Bressingham no time was lost and *Oliver Cromwell* was in steam and motion along a short stretch of track within only five weeks.

Oliver Cromwell has since taken its turn in giving demonstration footplate rides. Today there are a total of twelve standard gauge locomotives and in addition there are several narrow gauge locomotives hauling coaches on three separate routes totalling in all some five miles. On the 50 open days each summer, around 80,000 people of all ages take rides around the nursery by the lake or the woods. The 120,000 annual visitors can also see a collection of steam engines – some in motion – as well as a large museum housing a Royal Coach together with many items of railway interest. What began as Alan Bloom's hobby in 1961 has truly become the most comprehensive live steam museum in Europe.

BR Standard Class 7 Pacific locomotive no 70013, Oliver Cromwell, *admired by onlookers outside Norwich station, August 1968, during a break in its journey from Carlisle to Bressingham. (Photographed by G R Mortimer – picture courtesy Alan Bloom, Bressingham Steam Museum)*

Chapter 4

YARMOUTH AND LOWESTOFT

Yarmouth

Yarmouth dates back to Roman times when forts were built at Caister and Burgh Castle. The town acquired the title Great Yarmouth from a charter of 1272 and throughout the years it has served as one of the ports of the East Anglian fishing fleet. Today it is more likely that visitors will see container traffic and also supplies destined for the North Sea oil and gas rigs. Yet it was Yarmouth's long and sandy beaches that were to eventually lure thousands of holidaymakers each summer and when trains reached the coast for the first time on May 1st 1844, the journey became a possibility for many more people.

The railway was a Yarmouth & Norwich Company enterprise which provided a route from Norwich via Reedham and the chairman of the company was none other than George Stephenson himself with his son Robert as engineer. When a formal opening took place on April 30th 1844, a 14-coach special train left Norwich at 10.30 am with a brass band in the coach next to the engine. A local newspaper reported:

Yarmouth first saw trains when a line from Norwich via Reedham opened on April 30th 1844. By 1877 Yarmouth had three main termini, Yarmouth Vauxhall, Yarmouth Beach and Yarmouth South Town. Only Vauxhall station, seen here on a quiet day, has survived. (Lens of Sutton)

'The engine gave forth its note of warning, the band struck up, 'See, the conquering hero comes', the engine moved forward in its majestic might . . . the hills reverberated its warning, while the puffs of steam, heard long after its departure, sounded like the breathing of a Polypheme'

At Yarmouth, after a 50 minute journey, there were celebrations in the Assembly Rooms where the dinner menu included, 'spring

Corton station between Lowestoft Central and Yarmouth South Town seen here soon after the line was opened in July 1903 by the Norfolk & Suffolk Joint Committee. (Lens of Sutton)

chickens, green geese, tongues, pickled salmon, plovers' eggs, jellies, peaches and ices'!

On the next day, public services began with seven trains each way daily. At Norwich the station site was near the subsequent Norwich Thorpe station (today's BR station), while the Yarmouth terminus later became Yarmouth Vauxhall (also today's station). The opening also saw the introduction of an electric telegraph, the first in the world to be used with block signalling, although in a primitive form. It was a Cooke and Wheatstone system which at the same time could be used by members of the public to send messages, initially at 4/6d including delivery (22½p) but later reduced to 2/6d (12½p).

From June 1st 1859 Yarmouth had the benefit of a second rail route to London using the East Suffolk line via Haddiscoe and Beccles. The terminus was Yarmouth South Town sited across Breydon Water from the original (Vauxhall) station. The local newspapers were quick to praise the line for its punctuality and its spacious coaches. Trains from Ipswich divided at Beccles for Lowestoft and Yarmouth. When a curve was opened at Haddiscoe in June 1872 linking the two tracks, a service was possible between Yarmouth and Lowestoft via St. Olaves. Four trains were run each way daily except Wednesday when there were three.

Meantime on August 7th 1877 a rival company, the Yarmouth & Stalham (Light) Railway – later to become part of the M&GN system – opened a station to be called Yarmouth Beach, to the north of Vauxhall station. By 1883 trains from Yarmouth Beach were able to reach North Walsham and Melton Constable. The way was now open for holidaymakers from the Midlands and North to reach the east coast resort.

Almost 40 years after the first line from Norwich had been in existence, a second route opened via Acle. Yarmouth was increasing in popularity to holiday makers and also much of the steamer traffic along the coast from the river Thames was transferring to the railway. The new line, a shorter route, opened in two stages, reaching Yarmouth Vauxhall on June 1st 1883.

Yarmouth now had three stations serving different directions but two further routes were to follow. The Norfolk & Suffolk Joint

Lowestoft prospered as a seaside resort in the mid-1950s when up to 25 trains ran on Saturdays to and from Liverpool Street. DMUs bound for Ipswich and Norwich await departure at Lowestoft station, September 1988. (Author)

The 11.12 am Sprinter service leaves Reedham bound for Lowestoft, September 19th 1988. The station opened in May 1844 and in subsequent years carried a considerable trade in poultry and game. (Author)

Committee (a working arrangement between the GER and the M&GN) opened a line between Yarmouth South and Lowestoft Central on July 13th 1903 serving the numerous holiday camps and bungalow villages along the route and close to the sea. The importance of this stretch of nearly 13 miles increased when the M&GN opened, also in 1903, a connecting track round the inland side of Yarmouth to cross Breydon Water by means of a swing bridge and then over the GER route into Yarmouth Vauxhall and then on to the M&GN Beach station. At Caister Road Junction, the lines linked with a Quay tramway system.

During World War II on May 7th 1942, Yarmouth South Town station nearly suffered a major disaster when a 500 kg bomb fell on the track failing to explode. As luck would have it, a Naval Bomb Disposal Officer was nearby who was able to immediately defuse the bomb. In 1953, however, the station suffered badly when on January 31st the area was flooded and a signalman was trapped for 21 hours before being rescued by a boat. For a week no trains reached the station. On September 21st of the same year, the Breydon swing-bridge was closed which meant that the connection to Yarmouth Beach station was lost.

St Olaves station c1910 on the line from Beccles to Yarmouth South Town. The station opened in 1859 for both local and exchange traffic with services also available to Lowestoft Central. (Lens of Sutton)

The year 1959 saw major closures around Yarmouth with the Yarmouth Beach (ex-M&GN) to North Walsham and Melton Constable line closing to all traffic on March 2nd 1959 and the Yarmouth South line to Haddiscoe and Beccles route (ex-GER) following on November 2nd 1959. All that remained, apart from lines still in existence today, was the coastal line to Lowestoft which survived until May 4th 1970. There was one further closure on January 1st 1976 being that of the tramway to the quays and fish wharf.

A number of relics along the old Yarmouth–Beccles line can still be found. Belton station has been lost to building development but at St Olaves, the station sign can now be seen on the wall of St Olaves Service Station on the main road. The station site is today a residential area although, appropriately perhaps, in September 1988 one of the bungalows was occupied by 'Eddie' Stimpson, at one time the local station-master.

Lowestoft

Much of Lowestoft's early development was due to the well known contractor Sir Samuel Peto who owned the Norwich & Lowestoft Navigation, built the 1844 Yarmouth–Norwich line and then linked it to Lowestoft via Reedham. When rival railway systems frustrated plans for a major route westwards, Peto struck south giving Lowestoft a second route. This was the Lowestoft & Beccles Railway, which opened on June 1st 1859, leaving the town from Lowestoft Central station over a swing bridge at Oulton Broad (originally named Carlton Colville) making for Beccles and beyond. Initially the company had planned a terminus at South Lowestoft but this idea had been dropped. Instead the site was developed as a goods yard linking with South Side docks and there was also a branch to a coal and goods depot at Kirkley.

The port of Lowestoft grew rapidly from 1848, the year it had first come into railway hands. In less than a century it grew to an area of 74 acres which included well over 6,000 feet of quay handling various commodities plus nearly 4,500 feet of quay linked to the fishing industry. As herring catches from the North Sea swelled the trawlers' nets, the fish were landed, sold and packed in ice for despatch by rail inland. In the early part of this century, between 50,000 and 60,000 tons of fish were being landed annually, valued at over £500,000, of which the majority left by rail for London.

Holiday traffic to Lowestoft prospered although not on the scale of visitors to Yarmouth. Towards the end of the last century, passengers for Lowestoft on the fast trains from London changed at Beccles but by 1904 daily non-stop runs were available from Liverpool Street to both Yarmouth and Lowestoft. Traffic reached a peak in the mid-1950s when up to 25 trains in each direction ran on Saturdays during the summer, including a holiday special for Gorleston.

When proposals were announced regarding closure of the East Suffolk line between Lowestoft, Beccles and Ipswich, there was considerable dismay. Lowestoft's town council chairman said that loss of the railways 'would have very serious implications for the holiday industries and it would be serious indeed for the string of holiday camps along the coast.' A county council alderman said that closure would have an effect on the status and industrial life of the town claiming that they were isolated enough already. The strenuous efforts to save the line were rewarded when in July 1966, Minister of Transport, Mrs Barbara Castle, agreed that the line from Lowestoft to Ipswich should remain open.

In 1970 the line from Yarmouth closed but Lowestoft retained

All that remains of St Olaves station today is the name-plate fixed to the wall of St Olaves Service Station on the main road. The station area was demolished to make way for housing development. (Author)

38

its two routes to Norwich and Ipswich. These separated at Oulton Broad North junction where the Ipswich route crossed the waterway by a swing-bridge beyond which was once the connection to the old Kirkley goods depot.

Across the river Waveney, Haddiscoe station still serves the Lowestoft–Norwich line and the earlier Haddiscoe High Level station could still be found. Perched on an embankment close to where tracks once crossed, the platforms and basic platform building were almost overgrown, although to the north the signalbox has been tastefully converted and extended to become a private residence. From near the signal box it was possible to look out over the river Waveney to the buttresses that once supported a swing bridge. The original Low Level station was further to the north but in 1904 this became a goods depot and the present Haddiscoe station came into existence. At the same time, Haddiscoe High Level acquired its name having previously been known as Herringfleet Exchange station.

Standing not long ago at the present (low level) station on a warm September evening, it was difficult to imagine how any worthwhile passenger traffic could be found at a spot so far from habitation and so utterly isolated.

The northern rest pier of Beccles Swing Bridge across the river Waveney on the line from Beccles to Yarmouth photographed on December 19th 1961. Trains crossed at walking pace and until 1927 required pilotmen on the footplate. The line closed in 1959. (John H Meredith)

Chapter 5

GER TRACKS AROUND NORWICH

Wymondham to Fakenham

Anyone visiting Dereham station might be surprised to find the station buildings and platforms intact, track still in situ and clear evidence where extensive sidings once existed. Today the station building is a showroom for kitchens and bathrooms and the track, a link between Wymondham and a grainhead at North Elmham, is only little used. Occasional timber traffic still leaves Elmham and some fertiliser is brought in.

Yet certain parties regard parts of this line with interest. At Wymondham, still a BR station, David Turner has acquired the platform buildings and has plans to restore the site to include a tea room and, if possible, arrange a grand steam opening. In addition, the Wymondham–Dereham Rail Action Committee would like to see the line between Wymondham and Dereham, closed to passengers in 1969, reopened with a regular passenger service once again.

At County School, once a remote station mostly serving the nearby Watts Naval Training College (a Dr Barnardo's institution from 1901 to 1954), further interesting plans are afoot. The Fakenham & Dereham Railway Society has now been established for some years during which time part of the station at County School plus two platforms have been leased to them by the Breckland District Council. The station is to become a Heritage Centre and picnic area. With help from Manpower Services, much of the site has been cleared and by the end of 1988 a quantity of redundant track had been obtained from a Norwich siding. Already

Norwich Victoria station, seen here some years after closure to passengers in May 1916 looking rather the worse for wear. The terminus was once part of the original Eastern Union line to Norwich which opened in December 1849. (Lens of Sutton)

the society owns a Ruston 0-4-0 diesel locomotive plus 'Toby', a 'coffee pot' tram with a vertical boiler, from Belgium. The line will be known as the Wensum Valley Railway.

Yaxham station between Wymondham and Dereham remains in a well preserved state. The line closed to passengers in October 1969 although a single line has survived terminating at North Elmham for freight purposes. (Author)

Hopes are to additionally acquire a 'Toad' brake van in the near future and to lay about half-a-mile of track. Longer term thoughts include the possibility of an extension through Sennowe Park towards Great Ryburgh and also to lay track southwards to North Elmham. Should BR passenger trains ever reach Dereham again, this could considerably strengthen the society's aims as well as provide a very useful public service.

Trains first covered the line from Wymondham to Dereham when the North Norfolk Railway opened the branch for goods traffic on December 7th 1846 and for passengers on February 15th 1847. During the next year, a line was completed from Dereham to King's Lynn giving Norwich trains a through cross-country route to the latter. On March 20th 1849 a further branch connected Dereham and Fakenham yet it was another eight years before the Fakenham & Wells Railway completed a link to the coast.

Although the Norwich–King's Lynn route was kept fairly busy, the line to Wells was never greatly used despite a further branch opened in 1866 linking Wells with Heacham on the line from King's Lynn to Hunstanton. By 1880 passenger traffic suffered further when the rival Lynn & Fakenham Railway (later to become the M&GN) opened a line through Fakenham giving a direct route to King's Lynn. The company opened a separate station (Fakenham West) and there was no physical connection between the two routes.

Dereham station entrance in GER days c1905. The station first opened to goods in December 1846 and to passengers in February 1847 when the North Norfolk Railway opened a line from Wymondham. (Lens of Sutton)

Dereham station building is today a kitchen and bathroom showroom. In December 1988 the old waiting room, the single-storey building on the right, suffered damage by fire but the original station-master's house, the two-storey building, escaped. (Author)

At Fakenham (East) today there is a small estate of homes for elderly people where visitors might well wonder what a level-crossing gate is doing across the end of a short cul-de-sac. The homes covered the former station area and the level-crossing gate has been preserved as a permanent reminder of the past. Not far away can be found what was once the flourishing Great Eastern Hotel and almost opposite there is a small brick building which housed ponies used for occasional shunting in the adjacent goods yard. The sidings covered quite an extensive area flanked on one side by a granary and a malting on the other. These have both gone but, in September 1988, the small brick building had survived being in use as a workshop and office for furniture restoration.

Forncett to Wymondham

On May 2nd 1881 a loop almost seven miles long was opened between Forncett and Wymondham with one intermediate station at Ashwellthorpe. This was opened by the GER and it was intended more as a relief route rather than for local traffic giving through trains to North Norfolk the possibility of avoiding Norwich. The line, at one time double and of main line status, was also partly built to counter the M&GN encroachment on what the GER thought to be their 'territory'.

The line was never really successful. Had the North Norfolk coast developed to the extent the GER had hoped then it could have proved worthwhile. However, instead of the hoped-for

LNER class E4 2-4-0 (ex-GER designed by James Holden) at Fakenham East station in the 1930s. The station closed in October 1964. (D Thompson)

through expresses, for a few years around 1900 only a portion of the London–Norwich train was detached at Forncett to continue on to Dereham and Wells. Perhaps the line's greatest moment was when the 'Norfolk Coast Express' was diverted via Forncett and Wymondham because of floods putting the Forncett–Norwich line out of action.

The loop survived until September 10th 1939 for passengers and until August 4th 1951 for goods traffic. Subsequently part of the line near Wymondham was used for the storing of locomotives or carriages awaiting the scrapyard at Norwich.

Wroxham to County School

The branch from Wroxham to County School (on the Dereham–Fakenham line) was opened by the East Norfolk Railway in five stages from 1879 to 1882. Again there was competition from the M&GN with a line from Melton Constable to North Walsham running almost parallel to the north. At Aylsham there were rival

Very little remains of Fakenham East station. This brick building which once housed ponies used for occasional shunting in the adjacent goods yard has survived as an office and workshop for furniture restoration. (Author)

stations known as North and South. The town of Wroxham has boasted for many years that it has 'the largest village store in the world' called *Roys* and also claims with neighbouring Hoveton to be 'the capital of the Broads' with boats everywhere – on the river Bure and on Wroxham Broad itself.

The site of Aylsham (GER) station on the line between County School and Wroxham. In 1988 the Bure Valley Railway Company applied for a Light Railway Order to provide a 15 inch narrow-gauge railway between Aylsham and Wroxham. (Author)

The GER Wroxham–County School line was designed to link east and west Norfolk and also to prevent any independent company considering a line from Norwich to Aylsham direct. Aylsham, an important market town, had not been happy at being omitted from the original East Norfolk route and was a temptation for any such speculative promoter. Trains reached Aylsham from Wroxham on January 1st 1880 but the line's value depreciated only three years later when the Eastern & Midlands (later M&GN) reached Aylsham (North).

There were initially up to nine trains each way daily on the GER line but within a few years this fell to six. The line was hardly a success although freight traffic was occasionally heavy with cattle and later beet from intermediate stations at Cawston and Reepham. During the Second World War the branch assisted with traffic to RAF Coltishall.

The Wroxham–County School line survived until September 15th 1952 when it was closed between Reepham and County School. Eventual survival of the eastern section of the line was dependent on a link opened September 12th 1960, known as the Themelthorpe Curve, between the former GER and M&GN lines close to the village of the same name. The curve had the effect of reducing the round journey from Norwich Thorpe (now the BR station) to Norwich City from 64 to 40 miles with the haul via Cromer and Holt no longer necessary. Norwich City closed to passengers on March 2nd 1959 but continued for freight purposes

until almost ten years later. When it closed on February 3rd 1969 (the site became City Industrial Estate), the line was cut back to Lenwade where a 'One Train' single line light railway continued for a number of years to serve a local firm specialising in prefabricated housing sections and concrete girders.

Many stations along the route have survived the years mostly becoming private residences or offices. At Aylsham the former GER station stands neglected, not having been used by passengers since September 1952 and having finally closed to freight in March 1977. Yet at the present time there is a possibility of activity again!

The Bure Valley Railway Company applied to the Department of the Environment for a Light Railway Order early in 1988 and approval is expected early in 1989. The company is optimistic that work on clearance and tracklaying can commence in March 1989 with the intention of providing a 15 inch narrow-gauge railway service from Aylsham to Wroxham. Initially two train sets of ten carriages, seating 200 passengers, are expected to operate an hourly service during the summer months but there will be a limited timetable through the winter. The railway will be based at the GER Aylsham station with provision for a large car park, workshop/engine shed, restaurant and so forth. Halts are planned at Brampton and Coltishall and at Wroxham a station will be built adjacent to the BR station and a footbridge link provided.

The company anticipates that Wroxham could be reached by 1990. An enclosed bogie coach has already been constructed and this has been undergoing trials on the Ravenglass & Eskdale Railway in Cumbria. In due course it is hoped that two locomotives can be hired from the Romney, Hythe & Dymchurch Railway in Kent.

Chapter 6

NORFOLK/SUFFOLK BORDERS

The Waveney Valley Railway

Many relics of the earlier Tivetshall to Beccles railway line remain to be found. Tivetshall station buildings have gone – 'flattened almost overnight' bemoaned a local enthusiast – but, when visited, Pulham Market station was certainly still there. Indeed the owner, proud of his possession, was renovating the building much to its former standard. At the end of the platform stood the signal that in days gone by had controlled the branch out of Tivetshall. Only the arm was missing but this had been replaced by another from nearby Mellis.

Other buildings along the route were awaiting discovery. Pulham St Mary station building had been demolished in the 1970s yet Starston (which closed in 1866!) had survived as a private dwelling – totally overgrown and surrounded by trees. The building at Harleston, owned by a builder, still stood in the town but without its canopy. Further remnants of the line were easily found. Standing at the station building and platform at Geldeston, owned by an electronics company, it was not difficult to imagine the days of steam.

Beccles at the end of the line represented a sorry sight. From the days when it was an important junction with numerous sidings, sheds, four facing platforms and (in 1902) a staff of 55, there was only one through single line to be found and no staff were apparent. The island platform opposite was undergoing demolition

Starston station on the Waveney Valley line lasted only six years closing in 1866! The building remains intact as a private dwelling although somewhat overgrown. (Author)

and where Waveney Valley trains once called, weeds and rubble had replaced the track.

Early ideas for a line along the Waveney Valley were in 1846 proposing a route from Diss to serve Lowestoft and Yarmouth via Bungay and Beccles, giving the coastal towns a better service from London than was then possible via Norwich. This did not materialise and the townsfolk of Harleston, concerned that they might not get a railway, planned a line from Tivetshall Junction, to the north of Diss, direct to their town. In this way the Waveney Valley Railway Company (WVR) was formed with the company empowered by an Act of July 3rd 1851 to raise a capital of £80,000. Initial approval was only from Tivetshall to Bungay, a prosperous river navigation terminal and market town. It was not until two years later that a further Act of 1853 sanctioned the extension to Beccles.

There seemed little enthusiasm to proceed with construction and eventually a local committee was established in Harleston which managed to finalise a contract to build only from Tivetshall to their town. Lack of available finance meant that landowners along the route were asked to accept paid-up shares in settlement or rent out the land in question. Despite delays, Harleston was reached on December 1st 1855 and a service of five trains daily was established. The stretch to Bungay was held up because of labour and material shortages and it took a further five years to complete. Initially the EUR worked the line but by the time Bungay was reached on November 2nd 1860, the EUR had been taken over by the ECR, the latter promptly demanding 75% of the receipts and retaining the balance to clear debts.

A line from Tivetshall to Bungay was approved in 1851 but it took nine years to complete. Bungay station, photographed here in the early 1930s, no longer exists.
(D Thompson)

The remainder of the route from Bungay to Beccles ran into trouble when landowners claimed the WVR could not afford to complete the line. Arguments with the ECR persisted over working arrangements and eventually the WVR directors gave notice they would run the line themselves. The ECR immediately reduced its demand from 75% to 50% but this was rejected. Traffic reached

Beccles on March 2nd 1863 on the same day the WVR was formally absorbed into the Great Eastern Railway (GER).

Throughout the line's life there were four to seven trains daily each way. Yet the number of intermediate stations was not justified with Starston and Redenhall closing as early as 1866 and Wortwell in 1878. During World War I at Pulham Market a long siding was built to serve an airship base, an area which was used again in World War II by the RAF. The latter period proved the line's busiest time with Earsham alone handling some 200,000 tons of military stores to supply the numerous air bases in the area.

After World War II traffic declined to such an extent that passenger services were withdrawn on January 5th 1953 with freight following in stages to finally close on April 19th 1965.

At one time Beccles had four facing platforms, sheds and numerous sidings. Today only a single track passes through the station and the bay where the Waveney Valley trains called is now weeds and rubble. (Author)

Swaffham to Thetford

The town sign of Swaffham depicts a pedlar and his dog. There is a story from the 15th century that the pedlar had a dream that if he stood on London Bridge, he would meet a man who would make him rich. So John the pedlar with his dog hiked to London and there after several days met a shopkeeper who claimed a similar dream. The shopkeeper had dreamt that a pedlar from Swaffham had found a pot of gold in his garden.

The pedlar hurried back and there beneath a tree in his garden found not one, but two pots of gold coins. According to the records of the parish church of St Peter and St Paul, the pedlar gave much of the money to rebuild the north aisle.

Less fortunate were the finances of the railway companies which, four centuries later, found difficulty in raising sufficient capital to link Swaffham and Thetford. The first section of line to

Swaffham station, photographed in July 1964, closed to passengers in September 1968. Today the station building on the left survives as a listed building known as the Merle Boddy Centre. (D Thompson)

open was between Thetford (Roudham Junction) and Watton which began goods traffic on January 28th 1869 with passenger traffic following on October 18th 1869. The Thetford & Watton Railway (T&W) Bill had been approved by Parliament on July 16th 1866 with authority to raise £45,000 to construct the nine miles of track which would link Watton with the main line from Ely to Norwich.

The remaining link to be constructed by the Watton and Swaffham Railway was approved in 1869, the year trains reached Watton, with an authorised capital of £62,000. Nine and a half miles of track were needed to link with the GER line from King's Lynn to Dereham. With finance in short supply, it was not until September 20th 1875 that the line opened for goods traffic with passenger trains following on November 15th 1875. At the same time the T&W was authorised to raise £21,300 and donate £10,000 to the Watton & Swaffham, which it would now work. In 1898 both companies became part of the GER.

Prior to the First World War the area, known as the Breckland, was used for extensive military training with the transport of horses and large quantities of weapons and supplies by rail. By 1921, Roudham Junction, because of its isolated position, had lost its importance and main-line trains were no longer stopping there. The station closed officially on May 1st 1932. However, other stations were less neglected. In the years before the Second World War, Wretham & Hockham regularly won prizes for the upkeep of its station. When the war came, a RAF base was built alongside the track at Watton and a cement centre was established near Roudham for airfield construction.

After 1945 the line returned to a quiet role but, despite the use of diesel multiple-units, the Beeching Report brought services to an end. Passenger services ceased on June 15th 1964 although freight continued between Swaffham and Watton for almost another year with Home Hale providing useful sugar-beet traffic. Perhaps the line's best recollection for many was the station name together with an outline of a locomotive cut into the hedge by staff at Watton.

Swaffham station lives on today as a community centre known as the Merle Boddy Centre. It was opened by Gillian Shepherd MP on May 16th 1988 to be named after Merle Boddy, a Mayoress four times, who died in 1987. The listed building has been restored with the help of Manpower Services which at times had to have bricks handmade to match the existing ones from the last century.

Thetford to Bury St Edmunds

Travelling the new A45 bypass to the east of Bury St Edmunds (built on a section of the closed railway line from Long Melford), it is possible to get a splendid view of the fine station built by architect, Frederick Barnes. Its distinctive features are the two domed towers, one forming part of the station's arched frontage. Not far from the station can be found a 'Railway Mission' chapel where, earlier this century, the station-master and his staff attended worship each Sunday morning.

Towards the end of the last century there had been concern for many railmen who, because of their unsocial hours, could not attend Sunday services. In 1881/2, under the auspices of the Railway Mission, an inter-denominational body was formed. Worship first began in the station master's house, part of the main building. The mission prospered and it was not long before the Mission Hall was built. When officially opened on May 30th 1900, dignitaries present included the Mayor, Councillor Thomas Shillitoe and the GER Assistant Superintendent, R P Ellis.

Thetford Bridge after closure in 1960 when the Thetford to Bury St Edmunds line came to an end. For a time the building became a Youth Hostel but this closed in 1971. (Lens of Sutton)

The building, which still exists, has served many purposes. During the First World War it was a 'Soldiers' Rest' with refreshments available. Over the years its use by railmen has fallen away and one of its present functions is to attend the needs of the town's old folk.

The Bury St Edmunds & Thetford Railway Company was incorporated in 1865 with Royal approval to build the line of almost 13 miles granted in the same year. As with the line from Thetford to Swaffham, capital was hard to find particularly since it passed through some of Suffolk's least populated areas. When services finally started eleven years later, on March 1st 1876, the line was under Thetford & Watton working with a speed limit of 30 mph and a weight limit of 40 tons on locomotives. Officially the Bury St Edmunds and Thetford Railway terminated at Thetford Bridge to the south of the town although a spur to the north existed linking via GER tracks to the Roudham Junction/Swaffham line.

Financial problems continued and it was no surprise when the GER took over the line and cancelled through services north of Thetford. It was the two World Wars that eventually brought an increase of traffic with Barnham seeing much of the activity. During the First World War a large military camp was opened in the area and for the Second World War special sidings were built for an ICI factory with further sidings catering for one of the country's largest bomb dumps. The latter gave the line much traffic with wagons handling some 720,000 tons during the war years with many 'secret trains' leaving during the night.

After the war traffic reduced dramatically and on June 8th 1953

The derelict remains of Thetford Bridge station can be found in a council yard just below a roundabout where part of the trackbed was used to build a section of bypass. (Author)

passenger services came to an end. At Bury St Edmunds there were 'celebrations' to mark the end with a funeral (with coffin), a procession of 'weeping mourners' attired in Victorian dress, an old steam engine and a manual fire pump manned by 19th century firemen. Detonators were fired on the track, streamers were thrown and wreaths decorated the engine as the 'Thetford Flyer' made its last passenger journey.

Bury St Edmunds station in 1948 with its distinctive twin towers. An LNER 4-6-0 class B17 (H N Gresley), one of an early batch called 'Sandringhams', awaits departure. (D Thompson)

The closure of freight services in June 1960 finally brought the line to an end. Thetford Bridge station building became a Youth Hostel but this closed in 1971. In September 1988, the building lay derelict in a council yard almost hidden by trees and the nearby roundabout. Part of the trackbed was used to build about a mile of the new by-pass.

When on June 27th 1960, BR J17 locomotive no 65578 pulled slowly out of Bury St Edmunds station for the last time, pulling two wagons and a brake van, there was no big send-off. The *Bury Free Press* of July 1st 1960 reported:

'Few people in Bury seemed to know about the goods train. Pulling out of the station it was greeted with laughter and hoots of merriment from railway employees. Someone had chalked on the back of the brake van, 'This is the end'.

There were no other passengers except railway enthusiast, W F White, the Borough Treasurer, who was just going along for the ride – plus a reporter. At Thetford not a soul was in sight except 14-year old Patrick Spruce, a loco spotter, who had come to take pictures of the train he would see no more'.

Chapter 7

LINES AROUND CAMBRIDGE

St Ives to Huntingdon

Huntingdon, a prominent market and agricultural centre, first saw trains when the Ely & Huntingdon Railway opened a line from St Ives on August 17th 1847. Although the line terminated about a mile from the town, the station was known as Huntingdon. The GNR reached Huntingdon, closer to the town centre, from Kings Cross in 1850 and naturally called their station Huntingdon.

In 1851 the line from the 1847 Huntingdon station was extended to a junction with the GNR. Matters were further complicated in 1866 when the Midland Railway reached Huntingdon from the west to form an end-on junction with the old line (by now GER) near Huntingdon GNR station. In 1883 the town acquired yet another station (known as Huntingdon East from 1923) opened on the original line near the Huntingdon GNR station. At this point it was decided that the 1847 Huntingdon should be renamed Godmanchester to reduce confusion!

A feature of the St Ives–Huntingdon line was a number of weak wooden-built bridges crossing and re-crossing the river Ouse near Godmanchester. Only light locomotives could be used and the bridges remained a constant fire hazard from sparks in dry weather. The line had a speed limit of 40 mph but over some bridges it was reduced to 10 mph thus restricting the potential of the route. Just

One of the four wooden bridges crossing the river Ouse near Godmanchester on the St Ives to Huntingdon line photographed July 1962. Only light locomotives could be used and the structures were a continual fire hazard. (John H Meredith)

prior to the Second World War, Huntingdon (East) was busy serving both LMS and LNER trains but despite such activity the line to St Ives closed to passenger traffic in June 1959.

The site of Godmanchester station is today a council yard and car park. All that remains is a small cottage, probably a crossing keeper's lodge, immediately adjacent to a former level crossing. The wooden bridges over the waterways have all disappeared although a number of trestles can still be found over marshy ground near St Ives.

St Ives to March and Ramsey

The Wisbech, St Ives & Cambridge Junction Railway Bill was agreed in Parliament in 1846 and on May 3rd 1847 a line across the Fens was opened between March and Wisbech. On February 1st 1848 a line southwards from March to St Ives was opened, by which time the independent railway company had been incorporated into the Eastern Counties Railway (GER from 1862).

The route, described in an ECR report as 'one of the few railways originating with landowners in an agricultural district', failed to encourage much passenger traffic. As far as freight was concerned the line was soon to prove useful. Apart from the carrying of farm produce and, subsequently, considerable quantities of coal, it was also a means to avoid Ely at a time when the junction was generally congested with traffic from as many as six directions.

The GER was frustrated when Parliament agreed a line from March to Spalding which opened on April 1st 1867. The idea was originally conceived by the GER but approval was authorised instead to the rival Great Northern Railway. Many years of quarrelling followed, not to be resolved until July 3rd 1879 when the

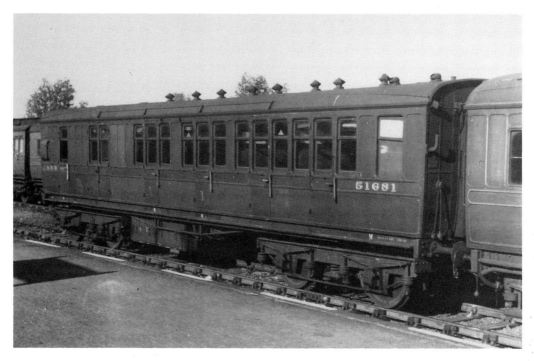

An ex-GCR corridor brake composite no 51681 seen at Ely on June 8th 1951. (John H. Meredith)

GN&GE Joint Committee was established. By this means, the GER was to eventually get its outlet to the north.

Meantime on July 22nd 1863 a line had opened from Holme, on the main GNR Huntingdon–Peterborough line, to Ramsey. Although the GER had a majority interest in the Ramsey Railway, the line was of necessity worked by the GNR. Even so, the GER remained concerned that this was a GNR manoeuvre to eventually reach Ely and so in 1875 had the branch vested in itself. As a double safeguard, the GER also gave successful support to the Ramsey & Somersham Railway, incorporated in that year. Feeling now secure, the GER passed the original branch back to the GNR on lease and did little to press the Somersham branch which did not finally open until September 16th 1889.

Ramsey, a town described as an 'island' in an otherwise totally flat landscape, had thus acquired two railways. A link between the two terminals was authorised but this was never put in hand. With the advent of the LNER in the 1920s, two lines to a relatively small location seemed unjustified with the result that the Somersham–Ramsey branch closed to passengers on September 22nd 1930. The Holme branch survived until October 6th 1947 although freight continued for a time afterwards.

The line from St Ives to March closed to goods in 1966 and to passengers on March 6th 1967. Much of the old trackbed can still be located although St Ives station was demolished to make way for a new bypass. For some years Somersham station remained intact with its awnings and old station lamps but this too has gone with only occasional footings traceable. Ramsey (east) station became a small industrial estate.

Newmarket & Chesterford Railway

The Newmarket & Chesterford Railway opened to goods traffic on January 3rd 1848 and to passengers on April 4th 1848. The line, which lasted less than four years, commenced from Great Chesterford on the Audley End to Cambridge line via Six Mile Bottom (then known as Westley) and then on to Newmarket.

When passenger services began there were six locomotives each named after famous racehorses. Yet the line was not to survive battles with the major rail companies. The ECR, hopeful of its collapse, declined all offers to lease or purchase since it threatened its own routes. Soon the Newmarket (as it became known) was suffering financially and, in the end, it was the ECR that helped to destroy the small company by operating at unreasonably competitive rates.

After further legal battles, the Newmarket eventually closed between Great Chesterford and Six Mile Bottom and settled for a link with Cambridge. Services on this route commenced on October 9th 1851 under ECR control. Within three years the new Cambridge to Newmarket line extended to Bury St Edmunds thus establishing a link between Cambridge and Ipswich which was to prove beneficial to the growth of both towns.

As anticipated by the original line's promoters, race-goers suffered lengthy delays at Cambridge and there were numerous petitions to re-open the old line. Even subsequent support from the Duke of York (later King George V), a great supporter of Newmarket Races, failed to move the railway authorities.

Today the Six Mile Bottom to Newmarket stretch is still in use but only earthworks and lined woodlands serve as a reminder of the earlier line. The original terminal at Newmarket, a highly ornate structure with corinthian columns, survived many years. It became a goods depot in 1902 lasting until 1967. Sadly, this well known landmark was allowed to deteriorate and in the early 1980s

A diesel shunter today at Ely in the bay where once trains left for St Ives. Passenger traffic on the line remained poor throughout and closure came comparatively early in February 1931. (Author)

suffered the indignity of demolition to make way for a housing estate.

Ely to St Ives

Stretham station, on the route from Ely to St Ives, closed to passengers nearly 60 years ago on February 2nd 1931, yet when visited in September 1988, the station building and platform looked as though it had hardly changed. On the side of the building, a notice still read YOU MAY TELEPHONE FROM HERE and below were two empty billboards which no doubt once accommodated details of LNER services and excursions.

Cyril Green, who occupies the station building, now a private residence, reminisced about the days when he started at Stretham with the LNER in the 1920s. 'It was a time when we had sidings and a signal box, and when trainloads of fruit pickers would arrive to be taken to their primitive camps in the nearby fields', he said, 'And the station yard was a hive of industry'. He added proudly, 'In those days I was the station-master, porter, signalman – in fact I did the lot!'

The first stage of a line from Ely to St Ives opened April 16th 1866 when trains of the Ely, Haddenham & Sutton Railway under GER operation reached Sutton. Initially there was little enthusiasm from the public. Soon after services began, a letter in the *Cambridge Independent Press* complained of the exorbitant return fare from Sutton to Ely and back which cost 2s 0d (10p), representing one fifth of the average agricultural workers weekly wage at that time.

The remainder of the line was completed some 12 years later on May 10th 1878 when Sutton was linked with Needleworth junction on the St Ives to March line. Throughout the line's life, passenger

Stretham station, not far from Ely, has survived the years as a private residence. When visited in 1988, the original railway employee from LNER days was still in residence. (Author)

traffic remained poor but seasonal freight traffic comprising sugar-beet and fruit proved useful. When closure to passenger traffic came on February 2nd 1931, nobody was really surprised and an alternative bus service was readily accepted. Freight survived for some years but eventually on October 5th 1964 the stretch finally closed. Today the track has gone and, apart from Stretham, many of the station buildings have gone.

Whilst seeking out Earith Bridge station, the author chanced upon a public house with a strange tale. During the First World War, the Crown at Earith was run by an ex-Sergeant Major Haver who had lost a leg during the Boer War. Early types of aircraft used the nearby airfields and the fitters found that a certain size of marbles could be used as a counter balance of weight in the planes' tubular frames. Haver, seeing a business prospect, bought up all the available marbles and sold them to the fitters – keeping his supply in his wooden leg!

Another of Haver's pursuits was to cross the Fen dykes and ditches by pole-vaulting but one day the pole snapped in the water. The weight of his leg full of marbles caused him to drown. In 1984 a wooden leg was found in a dyke – full of marbles. For anyone doubting the story, the evidence was there. The present landlord and his wife were clearing out recently when a jar of old marbles was found. Today it stands close to the fireplace as a reminder of the eccentric Sergeant Major.

Cambridge to Mildenhall
The GER line from Cambridge to Mildenhall via Fordham (on the route from Ely to Newmarket) was opened from Cambridge to Fordham on June 2nd 1884 with the final stretch to Mildenhall

Steam at Cambridge in June 1951. On the left, LNER 4-4-0 locomotive class D16/2 no 62543 and, on the right, class D16/3 no 62531 a later development of the same class. (John H Meredith)

completed the following year on April 1st. The branch was built to help ailing local agriculture and generally develop the sparse and thinly populated area; yet through most of its life it ran at a loss.

The line survived for passengers until 1962 yet efforts to economise had existed throughout. Towards the end of the last century, the GER used some of its obsolete locomotives and rolling stock on the branch but this had not always proved a saving when it came to fuel or repairs. In 1913, push–pull trains were introduced thus eliminating the locomotive turn-round at Mildenhall but these gave problems on busy market days when it was necessary to cope with additional passengers and extra luggage. Eventually the GER went back to standard trains using a conductor guard and, once again, using older coaches.

Mildenhall station, January 1962, where an LMS/LMR 2-6-0 H G Ivatt class 2MT locomotive plus passenger set await return to Fordham and Cambridge. (D Thompson)

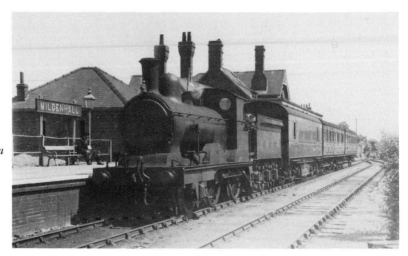

A member of staff enjoys the sun at Mildenhall as a GER 2-4-0 (J Holden) locomotive, LNER class E4 no 2783, with passenger coaches awaits departure in the late 1940s. (John H Meredith)

During the economies of the 1950s, British Railways introduced a number of fifty-four seat four-wheel railbuses which for a time brought new life to the branch. Yet even such increased efficiency did not stop the Mildenhall branch becoming an early victim of the Beeching cuts. Passenger traffic stopped on June 18th 1962 with goods traffic following within three years.

Mildenhall station in September 1988 as a strictly private residence. Passenger traffic came to an end in 1962 with goods traffic following three years later. (Author)

Much of the trackbed today has been ploughed over, yet a number of bridges still exist. Among the stations that have survived is Mildenhall, currently a strictly private residence. The property has been tastefully converted and the surrounding land developed into a spacious garden. The platform still exists and the old platform building carries many recollections of the past. Even the old booking office window has been blended into the present decor. Truly an idyllic setting for any rail enthusiast!

Chapter 8

SUFFOLK/ESSEX BORDERS

The railway along the attractive Stour Valley began its life as the Colchester, Stour Valley, Sudbury & Halstead Railway which had been agreed by an Act dated 1846. Initially the independent company, with an authorised capital of £250,000, had powers to construct a 12 mile line between Marks Tey and Sudbury, a prominent market and silk town at the head of the Stour Navigation. A further clause agreed the building of a line from Chappel to Halstead and at the same time powers were given to build a line from Colchester to Hythe. This would give trains direct access to Sudbury via the Colchester–Marks Tey main line for goods previously bought in by sea.

In June 1847 further Acts were agreed allowing the railway company to extend from Sudbury to Clare with a branch from Melford (Long Melford from February 1st 1884) to Bury St Edmunds. At the same time, the company was authorised to lease the whole of its undertaking to the Ipswich & Bury St Edmunds Railway which was absorbed by the Eastern Union Railway (EUR) the following month.

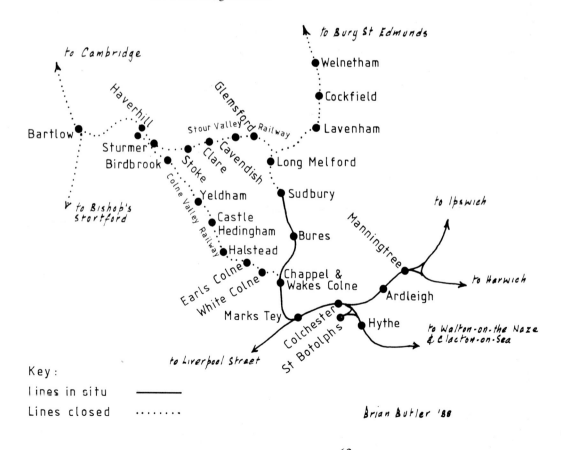

Key:
lines in situ ————
Lines closed ....

Brian Butler '88

In order that the Marks Tey to Sudbury branch could cross the narrow valley of the river Colne before climbing steeply towards the Mount Bures summit, a viaduct some 70 feet high had to be built. It was originally intended that the Chappel Viaduct should be of timber construction probably on brick piers but plans were changed when it was discovered that bricks could be made locally and cheaply at Bures.

Since there had been no ceremonial cutting of the first sod for the line to Sudbury, the laying of a foundation stone for the viaduct became quite an occasion. On the day, September 14th 1847, a procession emerged from a marquee headed by a band and a party of navvies. They were followed by the master of the works carrying on a cushion two silver trowels to be used by the Chairman and Vice-Chairman. Before the stone was laid, a bottle containing

Glemsford on the Stour Valley line which closed to passengers in March 1967. Many station buildings along this attractive route have today been converted to private properties. (Lens of Sutton)

Clare station before closure in 1967. The station building and platforms have today been splendidly incorporated within a country park centre surrounded by lawns. (Lens of Sutton)

Near the preserved station of Clare, a goods shed plus a short section of track remain. Inside the shed there are various railway relics on display. (Author)

coins of the day was placed under it but, within hours, the stone was removed and the coins taken away. Were it not for the keen eyes of a barmaid at the nearby *Rose and Crown* who spotted a new coin, the culprit, a Norwich bricklayer, might have got away with it.

The line from Marks Tey to Sudbury opened on July 2nd 1849. There were crossing loops at the intermediate stations of Chappel and Bures. When the first train left Marks Tey, the locomotive dislodged the triumphal arch with the result that it carried the laurels and other decorations round its chimney and dome throughout the journey to Sudbury!

On January 1st 1854, the Eastern Counties Railway (ECR) took over the Eastern Union Railway. Meanwhile approval for the Stour Valley Railway to build the previously-agreed line along the Colne Valley to Halstead had lapsed. Instead a new concern, the Colne Valley & Halstead Railway, was incorporated by an Act of June 30th 1856 and given permission to build from Chappel to Halstead. After difficult negotiations with the ECR, it was agreed that a junction could be built at Chappel for a payment of £1,500. In 1859 a further Act authorised the Colne Valley company to extend from Halstead to Haverhill and by May 10th 1863 the whole section had been opened.

Yet another company now emerged, the Sudbury & Clare Railway, to make up for the omission of the Stour Valley company to reach Bury St Edmunds as approved in the original 1846 Act. By an Act of July 1860, the Sudbury & Clare Company was empowered to build from Sudbury to Clare via Melford. However, as soon as the powers were obtained, the ECR took over and immediately sought extended powers to build from Sudbury (via Melford) to Shelford on the London–Cambridge main line, plus a branch from Melford to Bury St Edmunds. At the same time, the Colne Valley company, anxious to be independent from the ECR, sought approval for a line to Cambridge and, in the other direction, a line to Colchester.

A bitter struggle between the two powers ensued but the Colne Valley Bill was rejected and, on August 6th 1861, the ECR received approval to go ahead. However, further changes were imminent and in August 1862 an amalgamation of companies including the ECR came about and the Great Eastern Railway (GER) came into being. The Act also renewed the authorisation for the proposed ECR lines to proceed, in addition to a connecting line at Haverhill between the original Stour Valley and Colne Valley railways. The first section to open between Shelford and Haverhill began services on June 1st 1865 with three trains each way on weekdays and one on Sundays.

The remaining lines from Haverhill to Sudbury and from Melford to Bury St Edmunds followed on August 9th 1865. A new two-platform station was necessary at Sudbury since the line had to be diverted in a westerly direction. The old single-platform term-inus became part of the goods yard and was demolished as recently as 1985/6 when a store was built on the site.

During the period prior to the First World War, the lines saw some of their best traffic with seven weekday passenger trains daily on the stretch from Marks Tey to Sudbury. There were through trains between Cambridge and Clacton via Sudbury and through carriages between Liverpool Street and Sudbury on four trains daily. The war brought little reduction in traffic and on October 1st 1914, Chappel was given the name better known today, 'Chappel & Wakes Colne'.

By the 1920s the familiar pattern of competition was setting in although rail traffic continued quite healthily for some years. Economies were effected and these included the removal of various signal boxes to be replaced in some instances by ground frames. Many excursion trains remained in existence but the through carriages from Liverpool Street to Sudbury gave way to a single slip carriage removed daily at Marks Tey.

A Birmingham–Clacton train hauled by 4-6-0 LNER class B17 passes through Long Melford in July 1955. (D Thompson)

Cockfield station on the Long Melford to Bury St Edmunds line which closed to passengers in April 1961 photographed in August 1988 from the adjacent roadbridge. (Author)

When the Second World War came, the situation changed dramatically. Passenger services were reduced although freight services remained active. When the allied bomber offensive began, the lines assumed new importance with airfields being established throughout the area. The line from Cambridge to Chappel & Wakes Colne took on extra traffic as rubble was carried for the construction of a new airfield at Wormingford. When completed, a petrol depot was built at Chappel & Wakes Colne and trains were bringing high-octane petrol for the aircraft twice daily. Troop movements also figured largely in the line's traffic and it was not long before 2-8-0 'Austerity' locomotives were seen in use. There were frequent delays because of air raids or flying bombs but no actual damage was recorded.

After the war excursion trains returned once again, mostly to Clacton, but there were also excursion services to other seaside resorts and London. Many of the old GER station nameboards painted in their familiar blue survived beyond nationalisation in 1948, some until the late 1950s. One still exists today – that from Welnetham, on the Long Melford to Bury St Edmunds line, but it is now located at the National Railway Museum at York.

Changes came when British Rail announced a modernisation programme. From January 1st 1959, steam was scrapped to be replaced by Diesel Railbuses and Multiple Units. Although passenger traffic showed some improvement, it was not enough to overcome the increasing losses being incurred on these rural lines. Nobody was really surprised when closure came on April 10th 1961 to the passenger service between Long Melford and Bury St Edmunds where traffic had become very light.

The passenger service on the Colne Valley line was soon to follow but not before sharp reactions were expressed. Haverhill Urban District Council sent a telegram to Dr Beeching protesting most strongly at the proposal 'to sever the town's rail link with

London at a time when the town was planning to expand'. Despite such efforts, the last passenger train ran from Chappel & Wakes Colne to Haverhill on December 31st 1961. When in April 1965 the British Railways Board gave notice of their intention to close the remaining line from Marks Tey to Cambridge, there was again a vigorous reaction.

Total closure was planned for December 31st 1966 but, bearing in mind the views of the East Anglian Transport Users' Consultative Committee, the Minister of Transport refused permission for the Sudbury to Marks Tey section to be closed because of commuter needs and also development of the town at Sudbury. With regard to the Sudbury to Cambridge passenger service, matters were further delayed while local councils considered the possibility of providing annual subsidy guarantees. These were sought by the railway authorities following examination of the track which was found to be in a poor condition. The councils were concerned at the high costs involved and, not unexpectedly, declined support. The line from Sudbury to Shelford closed entirely on March 6th 1967.

In 1968 BR again published proposals for the closure of the Marks Tey to Sudbury line following a decision from the Minister of Transport to discontinue its subsidy. Again there was a considerable outcry from the public and for some years no decision was taken. In June 1972 the Minister for the Environment announced the line would close in July 1974 if the local councils would not support continuation. However, in 1974 there was an energy crisis with the possibility of petrol rationing. The result was that, in the interests of the local community, the line remained open.

In August 1988, Sudbury was found to be in a very neglected state with weeds rampant along the track and graffiti 'decorating' the station building. For a time the building, overlooked by a new leisure pool complex, had housed a local history museum but this has gone following a fire and only the sign 'Sudbury Museum' remained. Despite talk of future electrification for the Sudbury branch, it seemed hard to believe anyone wanted it to survive at all.

Many traces of the closed lines can be found today. On the line from Bury St Edmunds, all three intermediate station buildings exist. Welnetham station building, now privately owned, has a short awning and the station wall is still in situ. The owner remarked on the splendid soil found in his garden. The station-master in his time had obviously tired of the local clay and had arranged for quantities of fine Fen soil to be railed in by truck to take its place. One of the perks of the job, he obviously considered.

Further south, the station of Cockfield has survived although in poor condition. The ornate cast iron toilet that once adorned the platform has been moved and this now stands proudly (as an exhibit only!) at the East Anglian Railway Museum at Chappel & Wakes Colne. Similarly Lavenham station building and a nearby overbridge have survived with the area now used industrially.

On the Stour Valley line, the station buildings and platforms at

Clare stand virtually complete, splendidly incorporated within a country park centre. Nearby is a goods shed and a short section of track and inside can be found a former British Rail box van. The shed is today a museum where many old local railway photographs can be seen. Many other station buildings have survived along the line, mostly converted to private properties.

A Long Melford train approaches Lavenham station in April 1961 just before closure of the line to passengers. The station buildings today are used as offices but the platforms have gone. (D. Thompson)

The closed Colne Valley line from Chappel & Wakes Colne to Haverhill has similarly left reminders. Earls Colne station buildings have survived and are used today by a local firm. Sible & Castle Hedingham station was purchased on closure by a local woodworking company and in the early 1970s the buildings were due to be demolished by a bulldozer to make way for a new warehouse – but this never happened.

Also in the early 1970s another group of dedicated enthusiasts obtained a lease on the vacant goods yard, goods shed, signal box and station buildings at an intermediate station on the surviving Marks Tey to Sudbury branch.

Both these events were to have far-reaching effects in the two separate areas in the years to come. No doubt in the past many thought that steam had gone for good in the Colne Valley or at Chappel & Wakes Colne, but they were to be proved very wrong!

Chapter 9

A LINE PRESERVED
AND A RAILWAY MUSEUM

The Colne Valley Railway

Were it not for the quick thinking of members of the Colne Valley Railway Preservation Society (CVRPS), then Sible & Castle Hedingham station building might have been lost for good. When the Colne Valley line finally closed to goods traffic in December 1964, the whole station and goods yard area at Sible & Castle Hedingham was purchased by a local woodworking firm. In the early 1970s the station building was due to be demolished since the site was required for a new warehouse.

Such was the good fortune of the CVRPS that when they approached the owner, he agreed to hold back his bulldozer – provided the society could remove the station within six weeks! The target was kept, the building was carefully dismantled – brick by brick. While it took only a few weeks to remove, the rebuilding on its present site took two years. Yet now it stands at its present site, externally exactly as it appeared when first built in 1861, today a busy station serving the preserved trains of the Colne Valley Railway.

The project came into existence because of a vision inspired by a walk by two founder members of the society along the overgrown trackbed of the former railway in the summer of 1972. What followed was ten years of relentless hard work by a dedicated group of enthusiasts to recreate what can be seen today.

The Colne Valley Railway, founded in 1972, can be found just off the A604 between Halstead and Haverhill. Hedingham station, photographed here in August 1988, took two years to rebuild after its removal – brick by brick – from the original site. (Author)

Hedingham signal box at the Colne Valley Railway, originally built by the GER, was formerly located at Cressing on the Braintree branch. Made redundant by BR in 1977, the box was moved to the CVR in June of that year. (Author)

The first task was to obtain consent for the various planning applications submitted. When agreement was eventually given, work began in earnest in July 1973 to clear the site of almost ten years of overgrown trees and shrubs. The first locomotive arrived in September 1973, an ex-WD 0-6-0 Austerity saddle tank steam locomotive, WD190, built in 1952, causing quite a stir as it wound its way through the quiet Essex villages in 'full steam' to its new site on a massive low loader. The 'driver', the Society's Locomotive Superintendent, made sure that the local folk knew it was there by sounding the whistle quite frequently!

The excitement was of course shortlived, for it was to be another two years before a locomotive could be steamed again. The society was fortunate being sited by the A604 main road for the appearance of a steam locomotive in an adjacent field aroused much interest and it was not long before a willing band of volunteers was available. During the following year, the Colne Valley Preservation Society registered as a company. The two founder members became directors and the band of helpers became members of the society. The project was truly underway.

It was at this stage that the station building at Sible & Castle Hedingham was saved. Rebuilding the station as an exact replica of the past was painstaking but the efforts were justified. The CVRPS consider they are the only private railway to have dismantled, moved and rebuilt a brick station area using voluntary labour only. Efforts to save White Colne station in the same way were less successful since the local people needed the building for a much-needed community centre.

During 1974, three more locomotives arrived plus the first items of rolling stock. At the same time, the CVRPS acquired some track which had previously been used at Sudbury station and track laying at last began. The society's efforts were rewarded when, by Easter 1975, about a quarter of a mile of track had been completed and

Chappel & Wakes Colne station on the branch between Marks Tey and Sudbury. The buildings are a good example of Victorian architecture and the station is today the centre for the East Anglian Railway Museum. (Author)

three points had been laid. There was great excitement when the first 'steam up' was possible, an occasion for which both WD 190 and 0-4-0ST *Barrington* were brought into service. Footplate rides were given and there were many visitors.

Progress continued with further locomotives and coaches arriving. A building was now required for the second platform plus a signal box. With no suitable authentic building still in existence, the society built its own utilising bricks and materials found from various derelict stations. Any remaining bricks necessary were specially made by hand to match the originals. The need for a signal box was solved when one became available at Cressing following electrification of the Braintree to Witham branch. With the platforms completed, the society acquired an ex-GER pattern passenger footbridge from Stowmarket station. It had originated in 1898 and matched its new surroundings splendidly.

In the early 1980s one of the society's last obstacles was overcome. When the line closed, the girder bridge over the nearby river Colne was demolished. One similar bridge remained, however, along the line at Earls Colne station, used by the Anglian Water Authority as a footbridge. Following agreement with the water authority, the CVRPS gained possession of the bridge on the understanding it was replaced by a new one. Following invaluable assistance from the army, the 507 STRE (V) Railway Engineers, the operation was completed. With the replacement bridge in place, track laying began once again.

When the author visited the Colne Valley Railway in August 1988, a steam locomotive was pulling passenger coaches laden with children and adults along half a mile of track. The station area evoked memories of yesteryear and the ex-Cressing signal box with its 20-lever frame stood proudly at its new site. Adjacent stood a permanent way hut, previously the crossing-keeper's ground frame hut from White Colne.

Apart from numerous tank locomotives, a good selection of ex-BR coaches and many vans and wagons, there were still further interesting items to be seen. These included a Pullman car named *Aquila* built in 1951 once allocated to the Bournemouth Belle service and later sold to the Venice Simplon Orient Express and another Pullman named *Hermione* built in 1926, which was for a time part of the Devon Belle service. On the main platform there was a historic gem. The body (only) of a former six-wheel coach dating back to the 1880s could be seen, built entirely of wood and thought to be ex-North London Railway.

Standing on the busy platform and surrounded by so many railway relics of the past, it seemed incredible to think that just over 15 years ago, the site was a mere path through the undergrowth.

The East Anglian Railway Museum

A visit to Chappel & Wakes Colne in 1989 could prove exciting for, if all goes well, the sole surviving class N7 0-6-2T locomotive no 69621 should return to steam. For the special event, it will probably pull two vintage GER coaches both built around 1880.

The locomotive was designed by the GER and built at its Stratford Works in 1924 soon after the GER had been absorbed into the LNER. This was the last engine ever built at Stratford which subsequently became a maintenance depot when the LNER concentrated its locomotive construction elsewhere. The engine spent much of its life in the Liverpool Street suburban area but in 1962 it was withdrawn and stored for ten years before being towed to Chappel where it has been completely stripped down and rebuilt to BR main line standards.

The Stour Valley Preservation Society was formed on September 24th 1968. Its intention was to preserve all or part of the line from Sudbury to Shelford which had closed the previous year. This was an ambitious project and, with funds in short supply, it resulted in failure and the line was lost. In 1970, with the remaining stretch from Sudbury to Marks Tey still under threat of closure, the society found it necessary to acquire company status in order to negotiate with British Rail for take over of the branch and the Branch Line Preservation Society Company Ltd was formed. The primary objective was to safeguard the Marks Tey – Sudbury branch although events were to prove that the line remained open. In December 1970 the society formed its headquarters at Chappel & Wakes Colne station where a lease was negotiated on the redundant goods yard, goods shed, signal box and station buildings.

In his booklet, *The Stour Valley Railway*, B D J Walsh writes that the derelict condition of the site provided members with major obstacles to overcome. There was no electricity and the track, used for the various sidings, had been dismantled in preparation for removal. What followed deserved much praise. Within approximately three months of very hard work, track and pointwork over a third of a mile had been relaid and a locomotive, 0-6-0ST *Gunby*, was hauling a contractor's van loaded with passengers! Within a few more months, further rolling stock and locomotives arrived, the main attraction proving to be the class S15 locomotive, no 30841. Financial assistance to restore this fine engine came from a wellknown Suffolk brewing company and it was fitting the locomotive should be named 'Greene King'.

Progress continued with buildings restored and part of the station building became a bookshop – to become a major source of income. The GER-designed class N7 was soon to arrive for a complete rebuild. Further items continued to appear, including the 2-6-4 tank locomotive no 80151, an ex-BR standard class 4 engine built at Brighton as recently as 1956.

The late 1970s proved a difficult time for the society. A number of the locomotives hitherto attracting attention, notably 'Greene King', went to other locations. Attendances at the station site

The ornate cast-iron toilet to be found by the museum's restoration shed and workshop (as an exhibit only!) came from Cockfield station on the line from Long Melford to Bury St Edmunds. (Author)

dwindled and membership participation lessened. However, the acquisition of a footbridge from Sudbury station in the early 1980s was a boost to morale since visitors could now cross the BR line independently and the expense of a BR crossing keeper was no longer necessary.

Interest was further revived when the society attempted to run steam regularly on the branch on Sundays. Plans to steam between Chappel & Wakes Colne and Marks Tey were declined by BR for various reasons, so interest turned elsewhere on the site. Track was relaid along platform 2 to allow steam running and, following the purchase of an adjacent plot of land, an engine restoration shed and workshop were built. The shed had originally been used during the building of the Dartford Tunnel. The site acquired its present-day name of The East Anglian Railway Museum in late 1985.

A general view of Chappel & Wakes Colne station and the East Anglian Railway Museum. To the left is the regular BR track and, to the right, 3rd class coach no 704 (LNER no 60704). Beyond the goods shed is the museum's platform 3 where steam rides prove very popular on certain days from March to October. (Author)

A signal box, a Grade 1 listed building, was rescued from Mistley station (on the line to Harwich) for the sum of £5! The box was fully restored to eventually control most of the signalling and the points at the northern end of the site. In 1987 British Rail agreed to sell the station site despite the fact that a pay train service still operated from Colchester to Sudbury.

Today Chappel & Wakes Colne is not merely a station and museum but also an active repair and restoration depot. Visitors can find, not only restored engines and numerous vintage coaches but see every aspect of repair work, manned largely by volunteers. In the station booking hall, visitors can enjoy seeing a Great Eastern Railway crest cast into the fireplace or, in the goods shed across the track, a wide range of fascinating exhibits can be found. When not in steam, the popular N7 locomotive can be seen in the restoration shed. Steam days are held regularly from March to October on the first Sundays in the month and Bank Holidays but on Wednesdays during August.

Whatever the future of the BR Marks Tey to Sudbury branch, whether it is eventually closed – or even electrified – one thing is certain. The enthusiasm that has made the East Anglian Railway Museum what it is today, will go on for many years.

Chapter 10

THE MID-SUFFOLK LIGHT RAILWAY

Had the original plans of the independent Mid-Suffolk Light Railway (MSLR) approved in the 1901 Light Railway Order been realised, then a link would have existed between the GER stations of Haughley and Halesworth plus a line between the intermediate station of Kenton and Westerfield, just north of Ipswich. In addition, the inhabitants of this very rural part of Suffolk would have had access to the coast by changing at Halesworth for the Southwold Railway.

Despite agreeing the physical connections at its stations, the GER was initially suspicious of its new neighbour, especially when the MSLR chairman, F S Stevenson, purchased quantities of Midland Railway stock. This aroused unnecessary fears that the Midland might be considering the development of Southwold as a possible future east coast port. Yet the GER need not have concerned itself.

Construction of the MSLR began in May 1902 when the Duke of Cambridge cut the first sod at Westerfield at a ceremony which included over six hundred guests. Ironically this section of the line was never to be built. In addition it was soon discovered that marshland on the east–west stretch made it impossible to reach Halesworth from Laxfield. There were also serious financial problems since the project, estimated at £300,000 for the 42 miles of track, ran out of money during the first two years of construction.

LNER (ex-GER) 0-6-0 J15 no 65447 leaves Haughley with a mixed passenger/goods set in the early 1950s not long before closure of the MSLR. (Lens of Sutton)

Hudswell-Clarke 0-6-OT locomotive no 2 on the Mid Suffolk Light Railway approaches Mendlesham bound for Laxfield, probably 1908. The line was originally planned to reach Halesworth on the East Suffolk route but this never materialised. (Lens of Sutton)

There was further embarrassment when the County Council refused a loan which caused delays to the implementation of a goods service.

Hopes still existed to reach Halesworth across the marshland but subsequent deviation routes proved unsuccessful. Similarly the branch northwards from Westerfield to Kenton failed and only 2½ miles between Kenton and Debenham were completed. Considerable earthworks had been involved and although some goods trains became available, the service did not last.

Eventually on September 20th 1904, a goods service commenced over the 19 miles from Haughley to Laxfield. Small 0-6-0T locomotives had been ordered from Hudswell Clarke of Leeds but when the first was delivered to Haughley, the manufacturers had obviously heard of the line's financial problems. The company kept the engine, named *Haughley*, chained and padlocked to the rails until the first instalment of the purchase price had been received!

Passenger traffic had been refused until the line was complete. Progress had been slow with any surpluses made needed to meet interest arrears rather than invest in new construction. During 1906 goods trains reached Cratfield towards Halesworth but by May 1907 all work on the line had ceased. The company was declared bankrupt and a receiver was appointed. With the company still anxious to commence passenger services, the board withdrew the earlier stipulation that the line must be completed and agreed services could begin when the track reached a sufficiently high standard.

Eventually on September 29th 1908, just over four years since goods services initially commenced, passenger services between Haughley and Laxfield began. Seven old Metropolitan District

Railway carriages had been acquired cheaply following electrification of that system. When the first train left Laxfield for Haughley soon after 7.35 am on the opening day, there was great excitement from the local people who gathered to cheer the event and enliven the proceedings with exploding detonators. One of the first passengers was Major Daniel, the Receiver. *The East Anglian Daily Times* reported:

> 'a good many tickets were taken, and passengers were eager to enter the train. Only a few minutes behind time the signal was given by the Laxfield station master, and off the train steamed to the accompaniment of hearty cheers from the crowds on the platform, supplemented by the discharging of nearly 30 fog signals. It was a beautiful bright morning, and the pleasure and satisfaction which these first travellers on the line derived from their journey was reflected in their faces'.

At Haughley the station master was ready to receive the train which arrived about three minutes late. Some passengers changed, many travelling on to Ipswich, but quite a number waited for the train back to Laxfield which left at 10 am. There were numerous intermediate stations which were mostly small structures of corrugated iron but at the two termini, Haughley and Laxfield, the buildings were covered with zinc-coated sheets of iron in a brickwork pattern and then painted to look like real brickwork.

There were two or three trains daily and this remained the pattern throughout the line's life with mixed freight and passenger trains becoming a regular sight. Freight remained a useful commodity and included such items as milk churns and boxes of produce which were generally loaded en route. Tuesdays were Ipswich market days and cheap tickets were available to encourage

Mendlesham station was nearer to its village than some becoming one of the busier stops. During World War II the station gained extra traffic from the Mendlesham air base. (Lens of Sutton)

79

On open land not far from the village of Mendlesham can be found an old coach. It is believed to be of GNR origin although now looking rather the worse for wear. Surprisingly many of its windows are still intact. (Author)

A train bound for Haughley arrives at Brockford & Wetheringsett station on the MSLR although the nameboard uses only the name Brockford. The waiting room served a dual purpose – it was also a telephone kiosk. (Lens of Sutton)

travel. Loaded cattle trucks became a frequent sight; traffic that had previously travelled by road to the railhead at Framlingham.

In 1909 there was a further attempt to link Cratfield with Halesworth. An earlier proposal to reach Halesworth from the south over Southwold lines had not succeeded and an application to effect a junction with the GER to the north was now considered. Despite the fact the MSLR was still in receivership, an Amendment Order was approved on December 9th 1909. However, the work did not begin and when the stretch between Laxfield and Cratfield was abandoned early in 1912, it became clear that Halesworth would never be reached.

During the First World War, there was an incident on the night of 2nd/3rd September 1916, when thirteen Zeppelins flew over East Anglia to carry out one of the heaviest raids of the war. Considerable damage was done to GER property, especially at

Stratford and Liverpool Street, but one bomb scored a direct hit on the MSLR track between Gipping and Mendlesham. During the war, the MSLR was under War Office control when the decision was taken to lift much of the disused track betwen Kenton and Debenham and also Laxfield to Cratfield. The materials usefully replaced worn track elsewhere on the line.

The drivers and firemen of the MSLR took great pride in their locomotives which were always highly polished, inside and out. The line continued to give a good service but costs rose and receipts dwindled over the years. When 'grouping' came in 1923 the LNER was at first reluctant to take over the debts of a line that did not pay. After lengthy negotiations, the LNER agreed to meet a proportion of the liabilities and finally on July 1st 1924, the line's independence came to an end.

Whereas changes inevitably took place, the LNER was anxious not to drastically alter the character of this rural railway. One immediate decision was to withdraw the MSLR's locomotives and introduce its own stock. Also former GER coaches were introduced to replace the MSLR's second-hand stock. A section of worn track was relaid and a number of crossing-keepers were 'retired'. It became the task of the train crew to open and close the gates.

During the 1920s bus competition and private car travel began to erode the line's passenger traffic. The loss was partly offset by increasing goods traffic with sugar beet a reliable source. Commodities brought into the area consisted of coal from the Midlands and mixed freight from Felixstowe and Ipswich docks. Cattle traffic for Ipswich was slowing down and by the late 1930s the special Tuesday trains for market day were abandoned.

In 1933 the LNER seriously considered closure of the branch.

Aspall station was set in open country and never contributed much to passenger traffic. To the left of the picture, Lens of Sutton's bicycle! (Lens of Sutton)

A proposal to convert the trackbed to a road from Laxfield to Haughley was considered. However, after careful costing, it was decided that losses would be incurred and the line was saved. In August 1939 there was another attempt to complete the line to Halesworth when the Minister of Transport was approached. The Minister pointed out that powers had expired some 27 years previously and that fresh approval would be needed. When war broke out the following month, the matter was forgotten but the line acquired importance in a different way.

With petrol soon in short supply, passenger traffic grew again although the greatest impact on the line was the eventual basing of American airmen at Mendlesham and Horham airfields. Equipment and ammunition soon became a regular freight commodity and to cope with the traffic extra sidings were constructed at Haughley. After the war, passenger traffic increased with school-children making their way to and from Stowmarket Grammar School morning and late afternoon. J15 locomotives stationed at Laxfield became common along the line and, as previously, a high standard of cleanliness was maintained. Crews were known to get out at intermediate stations to brush off any ash!

Laxfield station remained the terminus of the MSLR throughout despite attempts to reach Halesworth. Goods trains reached Cratfield in 1906 but further progress became impossible due to financial troubles and intervening marshland. (Lens of Sutton)

There were few changes when the railways were nationalised in 1948 and the Mid-Suffolk line was to survive another 4½ years as part of BR. During this time the number of passengers dropped and there were times when trains ran empty. Towards the end the line could boast only one season-ticket holder. When closure was listed from July 28th 1952, there was a strong local outcry but the years of near-empty trains had been evidence enough.

The last official train, the 3.55 pm from Haughley, was far from

After closure Laxfield station building enjoyed various locations and uses. It was 'found' by the author in September 1988 in the corner of a sports field at nearby Bedfield! (Author)

empty. The platforms and temporary refreshment room were packed. Departure was delayed because a connecting train on the main line had broken down and the 3.55 pm, hauled by J15 0-6-0 no 65447, finally left at 4.48 pm. *The Evening Standard* reported that 'villagers from miles around gathered to make the last trip on the last of East Anglia's 'puffing-billy' lines, the Mid-Suffolk Railway. Farm workers and railway officials alike sang Auld Lang Syne as engine 65447 set out'. It was not quite the end, however, for at Laxfield several hundred passengers wanted to return and a final 'unofficial' trip was made.

At Laxfield today there is little to suggest that the village ever had a railway. The station site is now a corporation tip, although the corrugated-iron station building has been spared. After serving as a pavilion in various locations, it was finally located in the corner of a sports field at nearby Bedfield, virtually intact. Horham station survived many years but that too has now gone – to a private buyer from Southminster in Essex.

There were unexpected finds on farmland near Mendlesham. Not far from the road stood an old horse wagon complete with a separate compartment for the grooms from days of rail travel. Less than half-a-mile away there was another discovery. On almost open land, looking rather the worse for wear, stood an old coach of GNR origin – still with many of its windows intact.

Chapter 11

BRANCH LINES OF THE EAST SUFFOLK RAILWAY

The East Suffolk Railway first came into existence under its initial title of Halesworth, Beccles & Haddiscoe Railway when it opened to goods traffic on November 20th 1854 and passenger traffic on December 4th 1854, linking the three towns. During construction, Parliament gave approval for an extension southwards to Ipswich, meeting the Eastern Union Railway at Woodbridge.

This was all part of Sir Samuel Peto's plan for a route from Lowestoft to Ipswich, recognising that the new line would provide more direct access to London than travelling via Norwich. Sir Samuel Peto, already well known as the builder of Lowestoft Harbour, was well aware that such plans could also further his own interests by providing traffic to and from the port.

In 1856 Peto joined the East Suffolk Railway with his Yarmouth & Haddiscoe Railway and the Lowestoft & Beccles Railway enterprises giving him the access to the coast he needed. The route southwards from Woodbridge was completed over Eastern Counties Railway's (previously Eastern Union Railway) tracks. When a through line opened on June 1st 1859, it was operated by the Eastern Counties Railway (ECR) which was anxious to protect its existing routes elsewhere in the region.

The first trains to run from Ipswich to Lowestoft and Yarmouth were decorated with evergreens. The local press welcomed the service and a report read: 'trains run with great punctuality, and all are loud in their praises of the excellence of the line, and the commodiousness of the new carriages and stations'. There were four trains daily dividing at Beccles to go on to the two resorts.

Marlesford station on the Framlingham branch which closed to regular passenger services in 1952 is today a private residence. Located just off the A12 north of Wickham Market, an old GER coach body can still be seen on the former platform. (Author)

to Norwich to Yarmouth
Haddiscoe Somerleyton
Aldeby
Oulton Broad Central
to Tivetshall Lowestoft
Beccles Harbour
Carlton Colville Kirkley (goods)
Brampton Blythburgh
Halesworth Southwold
Walberswick
Wenhaston
Darsham
Saxmundham
Framlingham Leiston
Parham Thorpeness
Marlesford Aldeburgh
Wickham Market Snape (goods)
Melton
to Ipswich Woodbridge

Key :

Lines in situ ————

Lines lifted or
closed to passenger
traffic ········

Brian Butler '88

With connections available to London, cheap trips to the capital
began every Friday. Incorporated into construction of the East
Suffolk Railway were also branch lines to Framlingham, Snape
(goods only) and Aldeburgh. All were opened simultaneously with
the main line on June 1st 1859.

Wickham Market to Framlingham

When trains first reached Framlingham from Wickham Market in
1859, church bells were rung throughout the day, a cricket match
was played and tea was provided at the Crown Hotel but there was
a problem when a porter fell in front of a train. Luckily the driver
was able to stop his engine before any serious injury was done but,
since the porter was also the leader of the town band, the concert
to celebrate the opening had to be cancelled.

The branch, over five miles in length, was built at an estimated
cost of just over £40,000 and initially the weekday service was four
trains each way daily and two on Sundays. Passenger traffic was
generally poor although when Framlingham College opened in

85

1864, there were fluctuating increases in traffic. Yet Framlingham became an important railhead with the station a major grain despatch point. Also in such times, it was a common sight to see cattle along the road from Laxfield to Framlingham but when the Mid Suffolk Light Railway (MSLR) opened in 1904, this traffic was lost (see chapter 10).

Intermediate stations included Marlesford and Parham. Around the turn of the century a seed mill and corn merchant's depot was established near Marlesford station and subsequently an oil depot was built in the area. Perhaps the station's real claim to fame was when the Duke of Edinburgh's train was housed in the sidings overnight on May 2nd 1956 during his East Anglian tour of that year. There was great excitement locally when a highly-polished B1 4-6-0 locomotive, far grander than anything seen for years, hauled the Royal Train along the branch. The only other locomotives of note were usually Claud Hamilton 4-4-0s which were used to haul occasional seaside excursions from Framlingham with Felixstowe a popular destination.

In the 1920s between Marlesford and Parham, Hacheston Halt appeared, serving little other purpose than to combat growing competition from local buses. Parham, which opened with the line in 1859, achieved importance during the Second World War when petrol and bombs were handled at the station en route to a nearby airfield. Wickham Market station is signed 'Wickham Market for Campsey Ash' although the reverse would be more accurate since Wickham Market is more than two miles from the station!

The Framlingham branch line closed to regular passenger traffic on November 3rd 1952. Speed restrictions and a badly-sited terminal station had spelled doom to the branch which eventually succumbed to road competition. Goods services continued for a further 12½ years with a daily freight calling at all stations except

Ex-GER 2-4-2T LNER class F6 no 67230 with mixed rolling stock at Framlingham on July 19th 1952 not long before closure. The station was once a major grain despatch point. (D Thompson)

The site of Framlingham station, August 1988. The station building to the left has become a showroom for quality British motorcycles where one of the station's original ornamental brackets can be seen. (Author)

Parham. The traffic, mainly of grain, coal and sugar beet, survived until April 19th 1965 when the line closed to all traffic.

Wickham Market, on the main East Suffolk line, was reduced to the status of an unstaffed halt on March 6th 1967 and the station building on the long down platform has today become 'The Old Station House Emporium' selling antiques and the like. The up platform is no longer used because of line singling and the shelter has gone. There are traces of bays and also ramps which were used during the Second World War to load tanks into railway wagons. Not far away on the A12 Marlesford station building still exists as a private residence. On the platform stands an old GER coach body.

Framlingham station building today exists as a sales outlet for quality British motorcycles. Andy Tiernan, the proprietor, took great pride in showing an old station pillar with its original ornamental brackets still supporting one of the original girders from the platform building. Locals recalled that when the engine shed was demolished many years ago, it was pulled down by a locomotive pulling a steel hawser which had been tied around the brickwork!

A Freight Line to Snape

The branch to the Maltings at Snape, just under 1½ miles long and built at an estimated cost of just over £10,000, was intended as a passenger line. An access road to the station was provided and timetables showed particulars but this did not happen. A station on the main line to be called Snape Junction was never built and all that materialised was a lone signalbox. Instead the line was used for goods only with the sidings at Snape Bridge used for delivering barley, coal and coke. Malt was despatched from the branch.

To link the quay with the malt store there was an internal narrow gauge railway system where wagons were hauled by horses. Shunting on the branch was also carried out by horses, in common with many goods yards in East Anglia. The journey from the main line to Snape, however, sometimes proved a challenge for the J15 locomotives which had to cope with a steep climb up to the junction above the river. There was often much slipping on the rails and, on the odd occasion, a second run at the ascent was necessary!

The line lasted until March 7th 1960. When it closed, 30 foot sections of rails from the 1880s were still being used. Traffic had reduced to coal and coke only although after the Second World War there was increased activity when rubble from London following the air raids was sent to Snape Bridge. Meanwhile the Snape Maltings achieved fame from another activity apart from being a haven for bird-watchers. The area had become known for its connections with the Aldeburgh Festival and the Benjamin Britten concerts.

Saxmundham to Aldeburgh

With a branch already approved from Saxmundham to Leiston, the people of Aldeburgh wanted the line continued to serve their town. The company agreed in principle and a meeting was held in March 1859 to discuss the details. Sir Samuel Peto agreed to bear the cost and said he would lease the line for 21 years. During this time he expected Aldeburgh to expand, thus the line would pay for itself.

The ESR had provided the initial 3½ mile stretch to Leiston at the request of Richard Garrett, an ESR director. Garrett was also owner of Leiston's world-famous engineering works established in 1778, noted for its farm and road transport vehicles. In later years, Richard Garrett Ltd produced locomotive parts for Beyer Peacock locomotives which were used worldwide. With good local employment prospects, Leiston had grown and by 1851 had reached a population of over 1,500 inhabitants. The cost of the rail link to Leiston was estimated at just over £22,000 and, when trains started on June 1st 1859, there were five each way daily with two on Sundays.

The extension of the branch to Aldeburgh (named Aldborough until 1880) was approved in April 1859 and services began on April 12th 1860. The town was provided with an extravagant station for the size of the branch, built in anticipation of the traffic to come. At the time, Aldeburgh was a small harbour and fishing town although it was growing in popularity as a resort with upper-class families.

An Aldeburgh train waits at Saxmundham station, July 19th 1952. Note the movable section of platform which allows road traffic to cross, also the lefthand (down) platform which has now been demolished and moved further north. (John H Meredith)

This LNER warning notice can still be found not far from the earlier site of Leiston station. Leiston closed in September 1966 but the Aldeburgh branch between Saxmundham and Sizewell has remained open for atomic traffic. (Author)

Thorpeness station on the Aldeburgh branch opened shortly before World War I to boost the line's traffic. In 1988, over 20 years after closure, the site could barely be found in the undergrowth adjacent to a golf course. (Author)

With the railway available, fishing greatly increased and, in the years to come, as much as 70 tons of sprats and other fish were sometimes despatched by rail in one day.

On August 1st 1862, the East Suffolk line and its branches were incorporated into the Great Eastern Railway (GER) which did much to encourage traffic with cheap rates and excursions. Even so, by 1868, Aldeburgh passenger services were reduced to four each way daily and there were none on Sundays. From 1906 there were occasional through coaches which ran daily to and from Liverpool Street. On rarer occasions, visits were made by the 'Eastern Belle' touring train hauled by a GER Claud Hamilton 4-4-0.

In an attempt to boost traffic, the GER opened a halt at Thorpeness where a garden centre and country club had been developed. Old railway carriage bodies comprised the booking office and waiting room but the halt was too remote from any

centre and, with Aldeburgh station also badly sited to encourage day trippers, traffic suffered. Despite this, the LNER (after grouping in 1923) continued through trains and excursions until September 1939 when war broke out.

During hostilities, an emergency timetable was introduced and through trains from Aldeburgh to London were withdrawn. Beaches were wired off and holiday visitors no longer came. Evacuees came to the area from London but they were soon to move on again when invasion seemed a possibility. From 1940, armoured trains toured the line, each carrying a 6-pounder gun from the first tanks used in the 1914–18 war. These lasted until 1943 by which time the Allies were gaining the offensive and Leiston station was handling airfield traffic.

Aldeburgh failed to develop as a major resort and with traffic limited it was soon apparent that the line was doomed. On November 30th 1959 the station lost its goods facilities and in 1960 it was only the impending construction of the Sizewell power station that kept the line open for a further five years. Despite many economies, the end to passenger traffic on the whole branch came on September 12th 1966 but the line between Saxmundham and Sizewell remained open for atomic traffic.

It was not quite the end for passengers, however. In June 1977, some eleven years after closure, about 120 rail enthusiasts took a trip along the branch. A special two-coach passenger train, organised by the Felixstowe branch of the East Suffolk Travellers' Association, travelled the line to Sizewell to celebrate the centenary of the railway coming to Felixstowe.

The possibility of re-opening the branch as far as Leiston has

J15 0-6-0 no 65459 ready to haul a passenger train from Aldeburgh to Saxmundham on July 19th 1952. The branch survived for passengers until September 1966. (John H Meredith)

been proposed on more than one occasion. In 1987 the Leiston and District Road Safety Committee, concerned at the increase in road traffic around the nuclear plant, suggested that passenger trains should once again travel the line. But BR dismissed the idea saying that such a move would require 'a massive injection of cash running into several million pounds'. One imagines that, with a freight line already in existence, this will hardly be the end of the matter.

Today there is little along the old branch to recall the past. At Leiston the old platform edge can be found and two old cast-iron LNER notices still warn 'Beware of the trains'. The railway cottage near Thorpeness is an attractive private property surrounded by a golf course. Possibly players over recent years looking for lost balls have been surprised to find the nearby remains of Thorpeness station platform in the undergrowth!

Chapter 12

A BRANCH LINE TO SOUTHWOLD

Had the Mid-Suffolk Light Railway ever reached Halesworth or had proposals to link Southwold with Kessingland and possibly Lowestoft come about, then the future of the independent Southwold Railway might have been quite different. Even so, the delightful yet eccentric 3 foot gauge line lasted some 50 years until April 1929 when its usefulness was overtaken by motorbus competition.

First ideas for transport to reach Southwold came in October 1871 when the Lowestoft, Yarmouth and Southwold Tramway Co Ltd asked the local Corporation for permission to build a tramway from Lowestoft to Southwold. Hitherto the journey to the town had been by horse-drawn omnibus from the railway at Darsham about nine miles away so the idea was agreed although it was stipulated that the tramway should be from Halesworth.

Lack of funds prevented any development of the tramway and it was not until October 1875 that public meetings took place to press for a railway. Southwold, a small fishing village and trading port on the mouth of the river Blyth, was increasing in popularity as a 'watering place' and wanted a standard gauge link with the East Suffolk line. At the meetings, however, local people were persuaded that a low cost narrow-gauge railway would meet their needs. Among those pressing for such a line was Richard Rapier from a well known Ipswich engineering company who had gained considerable experience of narrow-gauge tracks in China. A Southwold Railway Bill was presented to Parliament and agreed on July 24th 1876.

Before the Southwold Railway came into existence in 1879, passengers reached the town by horse-drawn omnibus from Darsham station on the East Suffolk line which was about nine miles away. (Lens of Sutton)

Thanks largely to the efforts of the Halesworth Railway District Circle, a redundant signalbox from Halesworth has been reconstructed in the grounds of Halesworth Middle School complete with accessories and a signal. (Author)

'Halesworth for Southwold', August 1962, where passengers from the East Suffolk line once changed for the narrow-gauge railway. Halesworth, like Saxmundham, had sections of movable platform which swung aross the line to form a level crossing. (D Thompson)

After delays caused by landowners, work on the line began on May 3rd 1878. Being a single-track 3 ft gauge line it was lightly engineered although a swing bridge was necessary at Southwold across the river Blyth. The day services began, on September 24th 1879, a luncheon was held at the Swan Hotel, Southwold. During the speeches, the contractor, Mr Chambers, regretted the delays and pointed out his disappointment over the apathy in the town to get the railway going. Certain people, he said, had done a great deal to cause problems and no good had come of it.

Trains between Halesworth and Southwold were initially four daily each way and the time taken for the journey of about 9 miles was 37 minutes. There were three intermediate stations at Wen-

haston, Blythburgh and Walberswick although the latter two were opened subsequently in December 1879 and during 1882 respectively. The Board of Trade had determined that the maximum speed along the line was 16 miles per hour. This was rigidly adhered to and Rule 92 in the company's regulations stated, 'No train shall be run at a greater speed than 16 miles per hour and the engine driver is liable to two years' imprisonment if convicted of so doing'!

Coaches were six-wheeled with open-ended balconies and lit by oil lamps. In the booklet *Memories of the Southwold Railway*, A. Barrett Jenkins wrote about a schoolgirl who apparently once lost her ticket and, since the lights were not very bright, she turned up the lamp wick to find it. This caused the lamp's glass to smoke up and the guard who collected the tickets did not notice the out-of-date ticked offered to him!

Inside a coach the appearance was much like a tramcar. The seats were of wood installed along the sides of the coach and covered with a strip of carpet. The carriages were considered airy and spacious and a local paper, *The Halesworth Times*, wrote, 'We trust they will do much to revolutionise our present stupid and, to unprotected females and sometimes males, dangerous system of railway travel...' It seems incredible to consider that the dangers of individual enclosed compartments have only fully been appreciated in the last decade or so.

The Southwold Railway initially possessed three small blue 2-4-0 locomotives which had been purchased from Sharp Stewart of Manchester. Within four years, finances became sufficiently difficult that one had to be returned to the manufacturers with the remaining two, *Halesworth* and *Blyth*, being re-purchased and

2-4-2T Southwold, *no 1, built 1893, prepares to haul a mixed load from Wenhaston station, one of the three intermediate stations on the line. Leaving Wenhaston towards Southwold the train continued close to the river Blyth. (Lens of Sutton)*

A train enters Southwold station c1910. Southwold Railway opened on September 24th 1879. It was a single-track 3 ft gauge line with initially four daily trains for the 9-mile journey. (Lens of Sutton)

leased back to the railway. The first locomotive was converted to 3 foot 6 inches gauge and subsequently sold to the Santa Maria Railway in Columbia. By 1893, matters had improved and a 2-4-2T was purchased to become no 1 and called *Southwold*.

Despite the fact that space had been allowed for doubling the track at some future date, this was never done. The line remained single throughout except for a passing loop at Blythburgh. In 1907 the swing bridge at Southwold was renewed at considerable cost. This included widening and strengthening the line to allow conversion to standard gauge at some future date, should the GER or, later, the LNER take the line over. In 1902 a Railway Order authorised an extension to Kessingland to meet a GER branch from Lowestoft and agreed conversion of the gauge. When an offer to purchase the line came from the LNER in 1923, the Southwold Railway turned it down!

Throughout its life passenger traffic remained light but there were occasional busy times. On August Bank Holiday 1899 alone, 415 return tickets were sold and 33 single tickets. By 1913 the number of passengers carried per year had increased to 108,677 and a dividend on ordinary shares was possible at two per cent. By the following year a branch was constructed to Southwold harbour but it came too late, for the First World War had countered all prospects of fishing. Also in 1914 a new locomotive, a more powerful 0-6-2T named *Wenhaston* was purchased.

After the war there was continued satisfactory traffic but costs were rising, leaving no room for renewals or expansion. In 1922 a further two percent dividend was paid but this was to be the last. The beginning of the end came in April 1928. Southwold Corporation allowed motor coaches to operate within its boundaries with

the result that the railway lost the majority of its passenger traffic. Rail fares were dropped from 2s.3d. to 1s.6d. (approx 11p to 7½p) for the return journey with cheaper rates during the holiday season but the competition was too great.

At a meeting of the railway company, the chairman reported that with bus competition the Southwold Railway could not go on without help from the Corporation or the LNER. This was unlikely from the Corporation who had brought about the problem and the LNER were now not interested in taking over an ailing company. Closure was fixed for April 11th 1929 with the last train due to leave Southwold at 5.25 pm and returning at 7.02 pm.

2-4-0T Blyth no 3, originally built in 1879, prepares to leave Southwold for Halesworth. The line closed in 1929 although the railway was not finally demolished until 1941 during the Second World War when any scrap iron was requisitioned under emergency powers. (Lens of Sutton)

A local paper of April 12th 1929 described the events on the day:

> 'Tragedy and comedy were mixed when scores of people gathered at Halesworth to see the Southwold Railway close down after a life of fifty years.
> When the frail train started its last journey its four carriages were jammed with 150 people. As the train steamed out, the little booking office was besieged by people asking for tickets as souvenirs.
> The train had gone only ten yards when a woman grabbed her small son's hat and started to collect money for the engine-driver. Everyone showered silver into the hat.
> On arrival at Southwold a wreath was placed on the smokebox of the engine. People did not know whether to laugh or cry, for the closing down of this railway had caused a great deal of distress. The employees, numbering thirty, received notice of its closing down only two weeks ago.'

The railway was finally demolished during the Second World War in 1941. Rolling stock was destroyed and oxy-acetylene cutters assisted in the cutting up of the locomotives. Any scrap iron had been requisitioned under the wartime emergency powers. The

main structure of the swing bridge had been destroyed earlier in the war during the threat of invasion. Sale of the scrap material realised around £1,500 which was held on deposit.

By the early 1960s the demands of road traffic required the bridge over the A12 to be dismantled and another bridge near Halesworth was part demolished. At about the same time, a liquidator was appointed to wind up the affairs of the company and distribute any monies available to those entitled. Final degradation came in 1963 when Southwold station site was compulsorily acquired for use by the Suffolk and Ipswich Fire Authority who required the area for a fire station. When a new police station and police houses were added in 1968 on the remainder of the yard, the old booking office finally disappeared. In 1977 the last remaining span of the old swing bridge together with the temporary Bailey bridge of 1947 were removed so that a new footbridge could be built on the original railway bridge supports.

For the nostalgic, the museum at Southwold, opened in June 1933, is worth a visit. Here it is possible to find many relics of the old railway. At the East Anglian Transport Museum at Carlton Colville, an old railway van can be found. According to records, it is the only piece of rolling stock to avoid destruction having been converted into a tool shed on an allotment. When discovered in 1962, it was returned to Southwold station yard where temporary repairs were made. When the police station was built it was presented to Carlton Colville museum for restoration and display.

At Halesworth there is no sign of the narrow-gauge line station adjacent to the standard gauge track of the East Suffolk line, although bridge abutments can be seen on the nearby B1123. Whilst visiting Halesworth, it is interesting to note the sections of movable platforms which once formed a level crossing for the roads now blocked either side of the BR station. There was talk

locally that these sections, installed in 1922, might one day find a place at the National Railway Museum at York.

Further items of railway interest can be found at Halesworth Middle School, not far from the station, where one of the station signal boxes complete with all its accessories plus a signal have been preserved in the school grounds. This large-scale reconstruction was very much thanks to the efforts of the Halesworth Railway District Circle which helped to make the scheme possible.

The Southwold Railway failed largely through the company's own follies. Had earlier offers of purchase been accepted, or had the harbour branch not been delayed until 1914, then it just might be still there today. With a little more imagination it might even have become a preserved line, and with such lines a certainty as tourist attractions, it could hardly have been a loser.

The last remaining span of the old swing bridge across the river Blyth was finally removed in 1977 to make way for the footbridge seen here in August 1988. The original bridge supports are still in use. (Author)

Chapter 13

LINES AROUND BISHOP'S STORTFORD

St Margarets to Buntingford

When the people of Buntingford realised they were not to be served by any main line, they pressed for a branch of their own. The Ware, Hadham & Buntingford Railway was authorised on July 12th 1858 and opened some five years later on July 3rd 1863, operated by the GER. Despite the title, trains never went to Ware. The company made its junction with the Hertford East branch further south at St Margarets in order not to upset a local landowner.

The 13¾ mile branch had more than its fair share of troubles. At Westmill, an Ely contractor built a bridge of low-grade timber and it rotted within five years. Another at Braughing failed even before opening. Heavy compensations were paid to landowners along the route and, had the ECR (later GER) not intervened, the line could have failed before it began.

A passenger train awaits departure at St Margarets for Buntingford in the 1950s. The 13¼ mile branch failed, like so many, through competition from motor cars finally closing to all traffic in 1965. (Lens of Sutton)

Undeterred by its early problems, the line grew in importance. There were six intermediate stations and the line was single with passing loops. By 1914 there were eleven passenger trains daily although goods traffic was less encouraging. There was residential growth in the area and from 1922 there were a number of through-coach peak-hour workings from Liverpool Street. The branch continued to flourish until the 1950s when private cars began to dominate. In 1959 single diesel multiple units were introduced but

Lifting track at Saffron Walden just after closure of the line to passengers in September 1964 and to goods in December 1964. Notice of closure had caused many protests from the townsfolk some of whom had marched with banners reading, 'Don't saw off our branch'! (Lens of Sutton)

by the following year many off-peak trains were cancelled. Commuters preferred to motor to a main line rather than lose time changing at St Margarets.

Passenger closure followed inevitably on November 16th 1964 with goods traffic ceasing almost one year later. The terminus at Buntingford became an office and, as time passed, sections of the trackbed were lost following roadworks on the A10. Truly the motorcar had won the day.

Audley End to Bartlow

The Essex market town of Saffron Walden acquired its name from the Saffron Crocus, an important industry from the reign of Edward III until towards the end of the 18th century. Saffron, still the symbol of the town, was used as a dye, a medicine and a condiment. However the townspeople realised by the mid-19th century that the main railway lines had passed them by and endeavours were made to put the town on the railway map.

The ECR had refused to build a branch so initiative was taken by the local Gibson family, wealthy Quaker bankers, who helped to finance the Saffron Walden Railway. The company was incorporated in 1861 but it was not until four years later, on November 21st 1865, that trains reached the town from Audley End on the main Bishop's Stortford to Cambridge line. Within another year, the line was extended to Bartlow giving the Saffron Walden Railway access to the Cambridge to Colchester route.

The company kept going but only with difficulty. Gibson's Bank gave frequent loans but in the end the company sought help through an Official Receiver. On January 1st 1877, the GER purchased the line outright for £70,750 in stock and continued to

run it merely as a country branch. Thanks to the railway, Saffron Walden survived as a market town with a malting and a cement works introduced in the 1870s. Until 1894 a through train to London was run, otherwise services comprised some six daily over the whole route plus a further dozen between Saffron Walden and the main line at Audley End.

Perhaps one of the branch's proudest moments was when the Prince of Wales passed through Saffron Walden station in 1884 en route for Horseheath Lodge for a day's shooting with the Earl of Fife. As the Royal Saloon, hauled by a special engine, slackened through Saffron Walden, hundreds of spectators cheered and the Prince bowed an acknowledgement from the window. Bartlow station had been decorated for the occasion and a large number of lamps had been borrowed from Cambridge. The platform had been covered with cloth.

In March 1957 there was a celebration when Acrow Halt, to the north of Saffron Walden, was opened to serve the adjacent engineering works of the same name. As an N7 0-6-2T hauled the first train into the station, the driver and fireman were each presented with a bottle of champagne – to be drunk after duties of course! Meantime push and pull services had been introduced for reasons of economy but these later gave way to diesel railbuses. The branch was losing passengers to the motor car and soon commuters were driving to Audley End to catch main line trains instead of using the branch.

When an inquiry was held to consider the line's closure there was a storm of protest from the townsfolk. At a resumed inquiry held at the end of 1963, demonstrators held banners reading,

'Don't saw off our branch'. Yet despite objections, and serious concern at the reliability of a proposed replacement bus service, the last train left Saffron Walden at 8.09 pm on a Sunday night in September 1964. Amid the noise of a railbus siren and detonators placed on the track, the train made its way back to the Cambridge depot.

A general view of Bishop's Stortford station taken from the south on February 23rd 1952. On the left an 0-6-2T LNER class N7/3 no 69713. (John H Meredith)

In the *Walden Weekly News* in 1949, somebody signed 'C.M.' wrote as under:

> If you ever come to Walden by the single railway track,
> You're advised to place your luggage firmly on the rack,
> And walk the two odd miles at a steady, easy pace,
> For it will prove the quickest way of getting to the place.
>
> There have been tales, perhaps untrue, of our own local train,
> When, all the travellers getting in and getting out again,
> Still found themselves at Audley End – the driver very kind,
> Had brought the engine home – and left the carriages behind!

Bishop's Stortford to Braintree

According to an ancient custom of the manor of Dunmow in Essex, said to have been instituted in 1244, a flitch of bacon is given to any married couple who, after a year of marriage, can swear they have maintained perfect harmony and fidelity during that time. The practice was revised in 1855 and in 1857, during celebrations, the Eastern Counties Railway offered day return tickets for the price of a single fare to the nearest stations at either Bishop's Stortford or Braintree with 'conveyances' to take visitors on to Dunmow.

It was to be another 12 years before Dunmow got its own station,

an intermediate stop on a line from Braintree to Bishop's Stortford. Trains had reached Braintree from Witham, on the main Colchester line, in 1848 and the extension through Dunmow to Bishop's Stortford followed on February 22nd 1869. Yet the Bishop's Stortford, Dunmow & Braintree Railway had got into financial difficulties even before it had opened. It was saved from ruin by the GER which absorbed the company in 1865.

The take-over gave the GER a useful link between the Cambridge main line and the Essex coast resorts. Even so, the line was hardly used for such a purpose except for occasional excursions from Bishop's Stortford to the coast. Much of the time the line served passengers to Braintree only while freight traffic comprised coal, sugar-beet and general goods. The line gained a measure of importance in the early 1890s by the frequent conveyance of the Prince of Wales to Easton Lodge, a station specially built near the home of Lady Brooke (later Countess of Warwick). Although the station was built at the expense of the Countess, it was also open to the public.

On November 7th 1910, a halt was opened at Hockerill, less than a mile by road from Bishop's Stortford station. Few people used the halt but it did prove useful in one respect since it was well placed for the 19th hole of the town's golf course. In 1922, the GER, still seeking to develop traffic, opened two further halts along the line. These were at Bannister Green (just over four miles from Braintree) and at Stane Street (near the area known locally as Takeley Street). Since the halts were very small, notices were placed in the coaches warning passengers not to alight until the guard had lowered a set of steps.

The line survived until March 3rd 1952 for passengers (except for occasional excursions) yet goods traffic lingered until final closure in 1969. By comparison, the Braintree–Witham section has fared well. Electrified in 1979, a mixture of through (or part) trains to and from Liverpool Street and local workings to and from Witham provide a useful service.

Elsenham to Thaxted

The Elsenham & Thaxted Light Railway was a relative newcomer with Parliamentary sanction given in 1906. The intention was to promote local interests and generally assist a depressed agricultural area. Initially it was intended to reach Great Bardfield and plans for a narrow-gauge 2 feet 6 inches railway were submitted. However there was concern over the difficulties of through working at Elsenham so standard gauge was adopted. Another five years passed before work on the line began due to problems in raising capital. In the end the GER paid half the cost and there was a large grant from the Treasury.

On March 31st 1913, the line was officially opened by Sir Walter Gilbey and a special train hauled by two *Jubilee* class R24 0-6-0 tank locomotives and carrying GER officials and press representatives left Elsenham for Thaxted at 1.25 pm. After speeches, the official party returned by train where lunch was served. It was probably the only time that a restaurant car was seen along the Thaxted branch.

Much of the inspiration behind the line had come from Sir Walter Gilbey of Elsenham. Apart from being a prominent landowner, he was also the founder of the wellknown firm of wine merchants W and A Gilbey. The branch soon acquired the nickname 'The Gin and Toffee line', partly from the Gilbey family and partly through the confectionery manufacturers, Lee's of Thaxted. Lee's played quite a role in the line's economy with the need to supply local shopkeepers until the factory closed down in April 1969.

It was a most unusual railway. There was a speed restriction of

Felsted station (spelled Felstead until 1950) on the Bishop's Stortford–Braintree line just before closure to passengers in March 1952. A two coach passenger set is hauled by a 2-4-2T LNER (ex-GER) class F5 no 67196. (John H Meredith)

25 mph, there were never any signals and level-crossings were ungated. Throughout much of its life elderly 6-wheeled coaches were used and shunting at the intermediate station of Sibleys was carried out by tow rope. There was a goods loop at the station and the locomotive manoeuvred wagons from the other track! There were also three halts along the line although passengers were usually few in number. Anyone wishing to travel beyond the branch had to rebook at Elsenham.

The line prospered for the first ten years of its existence and, after 'grouping' in January 1923, it became part of the LNER. By this time road transport was competing and the line's revenues suffered as a result. During the Second World War the number of trains was drastically cut but, by the time full services were returned in 1948, many passengers had forsaken the railways for private cars and road transport. Replacement of the uncomfortable 6-wheeled coaches with modern bogied vehicles did little to bring people back.

In April 1951, British Railways announced plans to close the line although it was over a year before this was to take effect. On September 13th 1952, the final down train left Elsenham hauled by J 69/1 class locomotive no 68579. The three ex-GER corridor coaches, decorated for the occasion with streamers, carried over 400 passengers and in the guard's van there was a black-draped coffin bearing the inscription 'Died Waiting'.

The Elsenham to Thaxted branch had the distinction of being one of the last to be constructed and one of the first to close.

Chapter 14

BRANCH LINES TO THE ESSEX COAST

Witham to Maldon

It seems strange that the section of the original Maldon, Witham & Braintree Railway from Witham to Braintree should have survived today to prosper with electrification, yet the line from Witham to the ancient port of Maldon closed to passengers in September 1964. The saving of the former was helped largely through the efforts of the Braintree/Witham Railway Campaign Committee whereas the Maldon section probably failed for two reasons. One was the early failure of the railway company to improve the harbour facilities and the other the fact that Maldon did not succeed as a coastal resort – particularly with Southend and Clacton not far away.

The Maldon, Witham & Braintree Railway company had a difficult start in life. Authorised in 1846, the ECR shrewdly agreed it could cross its main line, thus in effect creating two branches requiring reversal at Witham. Subsequently in the same year, after suggesting to the local directors that the line might not pay, it took over the small company after falsely promising high dividends. In addition the ECR's actions blocked a drain of traffic from its own line.

The Witham/Maldon line, opened to passengers on October 2nd 1848, was built very economically with timber used where

The Maldon, Witham & Braintree Railway opened in 1848 although today only the Witham to Braintree branch has survived. A GER 0-6-0 J15 plus passenger set waits at Maldon (Maldon East from 1889 and Maldon East & Heybridge from 1907) c1930. (Lens of Sutton)

Woodham Ferrers, seen here in GER days, is today an intermediary station on the single track line which provides electric services between Wickford and Southminster. A line from Woodham Ferrers to Maldon, known as the New Essex line, opened in 1889 to survive for passengers only until 1939. (Lens of Sutton)

possible instead of bricks. Yet in contrast Maldon East station was built extravagantly in the style of a Jacobean mansion with ornate chimneys and Dutch gables and, across the front, a nine-arch arcade. There is a story, quite unproven, that the station's splendour is due to the fact that the deputy chairman of the ECR, David Waddington, was an election candidate at the time it was built.

It seems that quite a number of men, most of them freemen of Maldon and thus entitled to vote, were offered employment on railway construction some time before the election. In order to keep the potential voters occupied, the station was made bigger and more elaborate than it need have been! The workers, who were dismissed shortly after the poll, were paid a guinea (£1.05p) a week and for their efforts they gained the nickname of 'guinea pigs'.

Daily services from Witham to Maldon varied from seven to nine. The branch encouraged market gardening and locally-grown peas became a speciality. Fruit growing also prospered with Wickham Bishops, an intermediate station, becoming a despatch point. Yet the line was not to survive. Closure to passengers came on September 7th 1964 with goods traffic following on April 18th 1966 after which time the track was ripped up.

Part of the trackbed became lost under the A12 Witham bypass but earthworks and bridges can still be found. The best reminder of the branch today is the former GER station at Maldon which at the time of writing is known appropriately as The Great Eastern Motel. After closure the building had become exposed to vandalism but it was saved in the late 1970s when it opened as a restaurant.

Woodham Ferrers to Maldon

First trains from London to Southend were promoted by the London, Tilbury & Southend Railway (LT&S), reaching there in 1856. The GER's need for independent access to the resort was not met until October 1889, when a branch was opened from its main Colchester line at Shenfield. Passenger trains reached Wickford on January 1st 1889 and Southend Victoria on October 1st of the same year.

Cold Norton station c1910 on the Woodham Ferrers–Maldon line. Despite the hopes of the railway authorities, commuters did not settle in this bleak part of Essex. (Lens of Sutton)

With its alternative route to Southend established, the GER became anxious to open up remote parts of southern Essex by promoting several new ventures. These routes became known as the 'New Essex' lines and one of these was a branch from Wickford via Woodham Ferrers to Southminster. This opened to passengers on July 1st 1889 and, three months later – on the same day GER trains reached Southend, a further branch opened from Woodham Ferrers to Maldon West. Soon seven trains daily were passing through Cold Norton to reach Maldon West. Beyond tracks went on to link with either the line to Witham or to the 1848 Maldon station. Maldon was renamed Maldon East on October 1st 1889 and became 'Maldon East and Heybridge' on October 1st 1907.

Through the construction of triangular junctions at Witham, Maldon and Wickford, through excursions from the Colchester line were possible but such traffic did not prove popular. Passenger traffic generally was poor and few London commuters were anxious to move to this bleak part of the county. By 1914 the number of daily trains had dropped to five and from mid-1916 to mid-1919 the line was closed as a wartime economy measure.

The 1920s brought the usual competition from the roads and two halts were opened to encourage traffic. However, despite economies which included conductor guard working and certain line singling, the line finally closed to passengers just after the outset of the Second World War, on September 10th 1939. Goods traffic survived until 1953 with the exception of a freight link between Maldon West and Maldon East which finally closed in 1959.

The line is another example of one failing where another prospers. With trains between Woodham Ferrers and Maldon today almost forgotten, the branch to Southminster flourishes with frequent electric services. Up to 20 trains daily ply between Wickford and Southminster, these including a number of through Liverpool Street rush-hour workings.

Wivenhoe to Brightlingsea

When the devastating east coast floods came on January 31st 1953, many thought that the opportunity would be taken to close down the branch from Wivenhoe to Brightlingsea. Three miles of the line had been washed away yet, following pleas to protect the interests of the town and the important oyster trade, train services were resumed by the following December.

Passengers wait (or pose?) at Maldon West station around the turn of the century. The branch from Woodham Ferrers opened on October 1st 1889, the same day that GER trains first reached Southend from Shenfield. (Lens of Sutton)

Railways were first planned in the area when in 1863 the Tendring Hundred Railway (THR) was authorised to extend its Hythe–Wivenhoe branch towards Walton from a point ¼ mile beyond Wivenhoe station. However, the intervening ¼ mile section had already been appropriated by the Wivenhoe & Brightlingsea Railway (W&B) for its Brightlingsea branch although construction had not yet commenced. The W&B defaulted so the THR built the short section itself with subsequent disputes with the W&B over costs and receipts lasting many years.

Maldon West Station

A further complication came from the Mistley, Thorpe & Walton Railway (MT&W), incorporated in 1863, which planned to reach Walton from Ipswich and areas to the north. There was concern over unnecessary duplication of routes planned between Thorpe-le-Soken and Walton and, in any event, progress was so slow that Munro, the contractor, was dismissed in 1865. Because of financial disagreements, Munro refused to go and the outcome was a pitched battle on April 11th 1865 between 50 of Munro's men and 60 Harwich longshoremen hired by the company to effect his removal! The new contractor was no better and the MT&W was dissolved in 1869.

Initially the Wivenhoe & Brightlingsea had been unable to raise sufficient capital and only when the GER (after blocking a proposed W&B extension towards Clacton) offered one-third of the cost, was the project able to go ahead. Built by Munro (more successfully this time), the branch, single track and with no intermediate stations, opened on April 18th 1866. It was 5½ miles in length with its route following the north bank of the river Colne to cross Alresford Creek by a swing bridge before entering the Brightlingsea terminus.

The line was worked by the GER for 40% of the receipts although in August 1876 there was a dispute and the W&B hired its own stock and trains had to terminate short of Wivenhoe station. In June 1893 the GER purchased the line outright. Freight traffic was restricted due to lack of harbour development because of inadequate depth of water and construction of the quay, started by the W&B in 1866, was never completed. However, the town

Southminster station, c1910, in GER days. Today the station is a terminus on the line from Wickford with a weekday service providing some 20 electric trains each way daily including a number of through Liverpool Street workings. (Lens of Sutton)

proved successful as a yachting centre and as a resort for day trippers.

The original Brightlingsea station with its overall roof had a very draughty reputation with the North Sea's winds circulating around the structure during much of the year. Little wonder the townsfolk were delighted when it burnt down on New Year's Eve, 1901! It was replaced by a simpler station which had the advantage of being adjacent to a fish loading dock at the end of the line. Passenger traffic improved with more day trippers arriving to enjoy the local amusements and occasional boat trips.

Despite much publicised special cheap day tickets and excursions to London, the W&B suffered the usual competition from the roads and the line eventually closed on June 15th 1964. Much of the trackbed along the bank of the river Colne can still be found, serving as a defence against flooding. Brightlingsea station has gone – the site today is used for a local community centre.

Kelvedon to Tollesbury Pier

The Kelvedon, Tiptree & Tollesbury Pier Light Railway (K&T) was authorised by the Board of Trade on January 29th 1901 when a Light Railway Order was granted. The intention of the line was to help local farmers during a period of depression, serve the local fruit growers and also assist the Wilkin's jam factory. A C Wilkin was one of the instigators of the scheme with the firm donating land for what became Tiptree station.

Services from Kelvedon to Tollesbury began on October 1st 1904 without any formal ceremonies. The GER, after some hesitation, worked the line, almost nine miles long and of standard

Maldon East station soon after the turn of the century. The branch closed completely in 1966 yet this unexpectedly grand building has survived, currently known as The Great Eastern Motel. (Lens of Sutton)

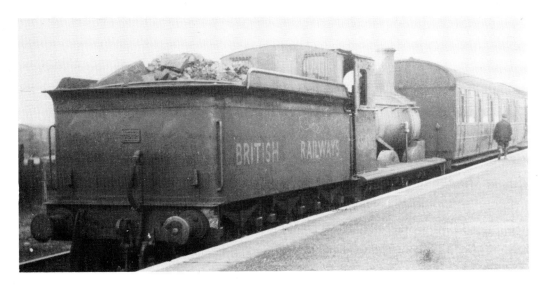

gauge. There was a speed restriction of 16 mph along the lightly built route, reduced to 10 mph 200 yards before any level crossings. When a J67 0-6-0T locomotive was employed during the early years, it was converted to a 2-4-0T by removing the forward coupling rods hopefully to reduce wear on the many sharp curves to be encountered.

Another purpose of the line was to assist revival of the ailing and isolated Tollesbury Pier. The line was extended to the pier on May 15th 1907 but little activity developed. The section closed after only 14 years use, on July 17th 1921, although during the Second World War the stretch usefully accommodated four WD locomotives with mobile guns. In 1940 the pier's track was removed and the pier isolated from the shore as an anti-invasion measure.

Initially carriages on the K&T had been four or six-wheeled stock, third class only and equipped with retractable steps since a number of platforms were almost at rail level. When the Wisbech & Upwell tramway closed in 1928, the branch acquired six further coaches. Two of these were bogie vehicles fitted at each end with balconies and wrought iron railings with gates. Two further coaches became available when the Stoke Ferry branch closed in September 1930. After refitting at Stratford works, they reached the K&T in 1931 enabling some earlier coaches, now 54 years old, to be withdrawn.

The line to Tollesbury closed to passengers with effect from May 7th 1951 although goods traffic continued for a number of years, mainly serving a fruit collection centre just beyond Tiptree. When the last train left Kelvedon on Saturday, May 5th 1951, it collected some 430 passengers in the three coaches during the journey. At Tiptree there was a black coffin on the platform covered with wreaths, one shaped with the letters BR. On the engine's smokebox was chalked 'Born 1904 . . . Died 1951' and on the bunker was the warning, 'There may be many a poor soul have to walk'.

Chapter 15

MORE LOST CAUSES

A Branch Line to Hadleigh

Hadleigh, in Suffolk, once a centre of the East Anglian cloth trade, first saw passenger trains on September 2nd 1847 when the Eastern Union & Hadleigh Junction Railway opened a 7¼ mile branch line from Bentley. The line was basically an Eastern Union Railway's (EUR) venture to block ECR progress towards Norwich and, at the same time, provide a possible through route, via Lavenham, to the Midlands. Not surprisingly the EUR took over the small company in 1848 although the furthest the branch reached was Hadleigh. The track was single although provision was made for double track plus a spur facing Ipswich in case the line ever reached further.

When a branch line from Bentley to Hadleigh opened in 1847, the Eastern Union Railway hoped to build on via Lavenham to the Midlands and also block ECR progress towards Norwich. Despite such endeavours, Hadleigh, seen here in September 1953, remained a terminus. (D Thompson)

Some two weeks after the line opened there was an unfortunate mishap. Despite the fact the station was still incomplete, an excursion had been arranged to take trippers to an annual regatta at Ipswich. Whilst a hundred or so people were waiting on the platform, a strong gale sprang up causing the newly-completed wall along the back of the platform, 14 feet high and 40 feet long, to collapse upon them. Nobody was killed outright but many were seriously injured.

Throughout the line's life passenger traffic was light. For much of the time there were five trains each way daily and three on

Sundays. Goods traffic benefited for a time while Hadleigh's milling and malting prospered. Further local industry included coconut matting, clothing and the manufacture of machinery.

By the present century, the town's population was falling and the isolation of the area from a main railway line discouraged growth. With buses established between Hadleigh and Ipswich by the early 1930s, the end for passenger traffic became inevitable. Closure came on February 29th 1932 although goods traffic survived until April 1965 with Hadleigh continuing as a useful agricultural railhead.

Quite a number of relics of the line remain. Raydon Wood platform and station building still exist at the entrance to a coal yard and Hadleigh station building comprises part of 'Wilsons of Hadleigh, Storekeepers and Warehousing'. The old station ticket office forms part of a weighbridge.

Diss to Scole

Not far from Alan Bloom's Steam Museum at Bressingham once existed another prominent market gardener whose foresight led to a prosperous business. When the Eastern Union Railway arrived at Diss in 1849, wealthy landowner, William Betts, saw an opportunity to get his produce speedily to the expanding London markets. By 1850 seven miles of standard gauge track linked the Frenze Estate at Scole with the main line at a junction just north of the present Diss station. Since this was a railway on a private estate no Act was needed.

At Scole the branch line served Frenze Hall, two large brick-fields and a barn. Two locomotives did the work, one a small 0-6-0 tank and the other a smaller 0-4-0 tank. There were no signalling problems since only one was used at a time. The locomotives filled with water from a tank which was replenished by pumps powered by traction engines. Betts had 15 wagons and, when these were insufficient, he hired further wagons from the ECR.

For many years Frenze Estate flourished. There were even times when a passenger service became available for the workers and a few local folk by using improvised wagons with planks for seats! However, when Betts died in 1885, all activity came to an end. The estate was divided and in addition renewals were needed to the track and rolling stock. Market gardening was discontinued and the line was taken up a year later.

The original station building at Hadleigh today where the old ticket office serves as part of a weighbridge. Passenger traffic had always been light and the line closed to regular passenger services in February 1932. (Author)

North Weald station, seen here in the 1930s and today a station on the Epping to Ongar Central line Underground system. (Lens of Sutton)

116

Steam from Epping to Ongar

Although today part of London's Central Line underground system, the line from Epping to Ongar takes its place as part of the GER's history. The ECR reached Loughton in 1856 but it was to be another nine years before an extension to the small market town of Ongar was completed, by which time the ECR had been merged into the GER. Traffic never reached expectations and no industries arrived to boost the traffic. The line from Epping to Ongar remained single.

Ongar station consisted of a one-side platform with substantial brick buildings. There was no canopy but a few seats and small areas of garden relieved the open area. A typical locomotive of the day would be a 2-4-2T F5 class often pulling just three coaches and destined for Liverpool Street. Other stations between Epping and the terminus were North Weald and Blake Hall.

The branch passed to the LNER in 1923 and later it became one of the lines to be taken over by the LPTB as part of the Central Line extensions. War delayed the completion of electrification and it was September 1949 before tube trains reached Epping. It took a further eight years before Ongar was reached, during which time vintage GER locomotives hauled coaches on a shuttle service.

Surprisingly there were no through tube services and the same shuttle service continued. As an economy measure, no sub station was built on the section and this meant that only specially equipped short trains could operate. A loop line, installed at North Weald, facilitated an improved service but it was found that two trains could not start simultaneously otherwise there would be an excessive voltage drop!

Mellis station on the main Stowmarket to Norwich line in the early 1930s not long before passenger closure of the branch to Eye in February 1931. On the right a branch train awaits departure. (D Thompson)

Over the years there has been talk of closure yet the line still exists. Blake Hall station closed in April 1966 and today only a peak hour service operates. The branch could perhaps be described as 'the line that might have been'. Instead it remains one of London Transport's rural single-line railways.

Mellis & Eye Railway

Standing today on what was once a road bridge over the railway at Yaxley (just off the A140), it is possible to look right across the fields and clearly determine where the railway track lead to Eye. The bridge was once known as 'The Duke's Bridge' for it had been hoped that the then Duke of Edinburgh might be available to open the line when services began in 1867 but this had not proved possible.

At the site of the terminus at Eye, the former station house seemed quite out of place dwarfed by modern agricultural buildings. The area when visited in August 1988 had become, it was claimed, the third largest chicken factory in the UK. The station platforms and buildings had gone but despite such developments, the station master's house still remained. When the site had been purchased, a life tenancy had been agreed for the railway worker living there and only in recent years the property, now in poor condition, had become vacant with the former occupant rehoused.

A station survived at the junction of Mellis, on the main Haughley to Norwich line, until November 7th 1966. The platforms and the tall brick 'Mellis junction' signal box were removed only within the past two years because of the electrification scheme in hand on the Norwich line and the level-crossing gate, much to the relief of local residents, has become automatic.

When in 1849 the main line to Norwich passed several miles to the west of Eye, the town's population suffered. An Act, promoted by local interests, followed in 1865 authorising a branch with a capital of £20,000. However, the Mellis & Eye Railway did little to reverse the trend. The three mile long branch opened after many delays on April 2nd 1867 when a locomotive hauled eight four-wheeled coaches along the line. The local inhabitants turned out to watch the event but there were few celebrations.

The railway continued a quiet existence and freight carried consisted mainly of coal and beetroot. In 1898 the company was incorporated into the GER and in 1922, in the hope of improving passenger traffic, a halt was opened close to the bridge at Yaxley. Matters hardly improved and on February 2nd 1931, the branch closed to passenger traffic. Freight services survived until July 1964.

There was little resistance to the passenger closure. The *Suffolk Chronicle & Mercury* of January 30th 1931, in giving details of the Eastern Counties buses that would take over, merely observed that as far as the railway was concerned, the town was being 'Eye solated'!

The Wisbech & Upwell Steam Tramway

Although a tramway, the Wisbech & Upwell Tramway is worthy of mention since it was basically a GER venture to assist agriculture in the area. An earlier proposal for such a link had come from a man called Gillard who obtained powers to build between the two places but due to financial problems the idea was abandoned. It was the GER in 1880 which resurrected the scheme but decided to cut costs by constructing a tramway to be worked by steam locomotives.

An Act was agreed in July 1882, construction began at once and in August 1883 the tramway opened from Wisbech (GER station) to Outwell. It is recorded that on the first day of operation there were 960 passengers. The extension from Outwell to Upwell followed in September 1884 giving an overall distance of about five miles. The track followed the bank of the former Wisbech Canal, much of it parallel to the A1101 roadway. In places the track was laid in the roadway, embedded in the surface so as not to obstruct road vehicles. Initially this was done with cinder ballast although in later years stones were used covered with tarmacadam.

The original tram locomotives were designed by Thomas Wordsell (GER Locomotive Superintendent 1881–1885) being 0-4-0 tanks. They had cow-catchers, warning bells and governors which shut off steam and applied brakes should 10 mph be exceeded. Enclosed in wooden casing, they had more the appearance of a freight brake van. Some of these survived grouping to become LNER class Y6. Between 1903 and 1921 a number of the original locomotives were replaced by more powerful 0-6-0T fully enclosed locomotives (GER class C53) designed by Holden (GER Locomotive Superintendent 1885–1907).

For the first year of operation four-wheeled carriages only were used but bogie coaches were soon to be introduced. These had end

platforms with ornamental railings and were provided with steps since the stations lacked platforms. During much of the tramway's life there were eight trams daily and as far as freight was concerned over 500 tons of produce was carried in the year 1888. Goods traffic varied according to season yet during the year 1910 as much as 14,549 tons was achieved.

Passenger services on the tramway came to an end on January 1st 1928 because of increasing competition from the roads. After closure, one of the bogie coaches found its way to a section of disused track near Camerton in Avon where it was used for the filming in 1953 of *The Titfield Thunderbolt*. Freight traffic continued for quite a number of years. Towards the end, working was by diesel locomotives but traffic continued to decrease.

Finally on May 23rd 1966, the last goods tram made its way along the track, accompanied by a convoy of cars. Three enthusiasts even managed to get a ride aboard the three trucks and guards van. *The Eastern Daily Press* commented, 'No one could have

described this as a memorable funeral for the 83-year old line, the last rail link of its kind in the country. The occasion seemed to give the curious, rather than the genuinely sad, an excuse for an afternoon out. The Wisbech–Upwell tramway went out of operation quietly and even a little ignominiously'.

The Wisbech & Upwell Tramway c1910. The original 0-4-0 tram locomotives were fitted with cow-catchers and warning bells and were enclosed in wooden casing giving more the appearance of a freight brake van. (Lens of Sutton)

CONCLUSION

The decline of many of East Anglia's lines began in the 1920s. Buses were providing a more flexible service than the trains and road haulage was on the increase. An early casualty was the narrow-gauge Southwold Railway from Halesworth to Southwold which closed on April 12th 1929. Other branches soon followed. 1930 saw the closure to passengers of the Stoke Ferry branch with the Mellis & Eye Railway and the line from Ely to St Ives closing the following year, although freight traffic continued for quite a number of years.

More lines followed yet during the 1939–1945 war many found new uses supplying the numerous East Anglian airfields with petrol or bombs. After the war losses increased and in 1959 much of the M&GN system closed altogether. In March 1963 proposals were made in a report which became popularly known as the 'Beeching Plan'. Basically the idea was to keep lines considered suitable to rail traffic and give up the remainder. It was claimed that one third of the rail system in Britain carried only 1% of the total traffic!

The resultant closure of lines over the next decade became almost a landslide throughout the region. Rail traffic fell dramatically with passengers and freight becoming almost completely reliant on road transport. Some routes survived, including the former GN&GE joint line from March to Spalding, but in 1982 this too was axed. Today the basic main lines of the past remain but the lives of the few remaining branches must surely be on a short term basis.

'The Norfolkman' and 'The Broadsman' may have gone, yet the diesels that took over from steam are themselves slowly disappearing. Electric services reached Norwich from Liverpool Street in May 1987 and more such plans are underway. Despite such advances however, there are numerous places where steam trains are not forgotten. To the south the Colne Valley Railway and the East Anglian Railway Museum keep alive such memories and to the north can be found the North Norfolk Railway and the Wells & Walsingham Light Railway.

The past lives on in other ways too. The Great Eastern Railway Society (GERS) was formed in 1973 to generally promote interest in the GER and encourage research into its history. There are over 600 members and many visits and trips are arranged. Publications include *The Great Eastern Journal* and *The Great Eastern News*. From an early stage the GERS forged links with the Passmore Edwards Museum at Stratford in east London where the society's records and relics are kept. This co-operation brought about the opening of the North Woolwich Old Station Museum, open seven days a week, where displays in the restored station cover the history of the GER.

The Midland & Great Northern Joint Railway Society was founded when the M&GN closed in 1959 so that part of that railway might be preserved for the 'pleasure, enjoyment and education of future generations'. One of the society's main roles is to preserve and restore to active use the locomotives and coaches which it owns. In addition many members play an active part in the day to day running of the North Norfolk Railway where currently the mainstay is the society's 0-6-0 ex-GER J15 class locomotive. Future plans include completion of the class B12/3 4-6-0 ex-LNER locomotive which, when fully restored, will prove useful when hauling passenger trains on the extended line to Holt. The M&GN Society produces a quarterly journal called *Joint Line*.

Yet, what of the future for East Anglia's railways? Is it possible that the ever-increasing fares will push many of the long-distance commuters off the trains? Although passenger traffic may suffer, there appears hope that certain freight traffic may return if the proposed Euro-Freighter can replace the juggernaut on our already over-crowded roads. With the European Open Market coming in 1992 and the Channel Tunnel planned to open in 1993, both these events are likely to have a considerable impact on the railways and the movement of goods in particular.

A further aspect of the future is the possibility that light railway schemes might return to revitalise a number of our inner cities. The current successes of the Docklands Light Railway and the Tyne and Wear Metro have brought about a flood of applications to build new systems elsewhere, including the Greater Manchester Rapid Transit, the Midland Metro and many others. Further places are being considered – including Norwich. Is it possible that the town which once boasted three terminal stations, will one day benefit from its own light railway system?

Back to the past again, part of an article in the *East Anglian Daily Times* of June 1st 1971 on vanishing branch lines read:

'For some people, the rural scene has never been quite the same since the branch railway lines closed. The little local trains chuntering fussily through the quiet countryside under billowing plumes of steam were an accepted part of rural life that is still sadly missed by many old enough to remember them'.

OPENING AND FINAL CLOSURE DATES OF LINES TO REGULAR PASSENGER TRAFFIC

Line	Opened	Final Closure
King's Lynn to Dereham	1846/1848	1968
Wymondham to Dereham	1847	1969
St Ives to Huntingdon	1847	1959
Bentley to Hadleigh	1847	1932
St Ives to March	1848	1967
Magdalen Road to Wisbech	1848	1968
Great Chesterford to Six Mile Bottom	1848	1851
Witham to Maldon	1848	1964
Dereham to Fakenham	1849	1964
Sudbury to Shelford	1849/1865	1967
Diss to Scole	1850	1886
Yarmouth (South Town) to Beccles	1854/1859	1959
Tivetshall to Beccles	1855/1863	1953
Wells to Fakenham*1	1857	1964
Wickham Market to Framlingham	1859	1952
A Branch to Snape (goods only)	1859	1960
Saxmundham to Aldeburgh	1859	1966
Chappel & Wakes Colne to Haverhill*2*3	1860/1863	1962
King's Lynn to Hunstanton	1862	1969
Spalding/Sutton Bridge/South Lynn	1862/1865	1959
Holme to Ramsey	1863	1947
St Margarets to Buntingford	1863	1964
Audley End to Bartlow	1865/1866	1964
Epping to Ongar	1865	1957†
Long Melford to Bury St Edmunds	1865	1961
Heacham to Wells	1866	1952
Sutton Bridge/Wisbech/Peterborough	1866	1959
Ely to St Ives	1866/1878	1931
Wivenhoe to Brightlingsea	1866	1964
Mellis & Eye Railway	1867	1931
Thetford to Swaffham	1869/1875	1964
Bishop's Stortford to Braintree	1869	1952
Thetford to Bury St Edmunds	1876	1953
Melton Constable/North Walsham/ Yarmouth Beach	1877/1883	1959
King's Lynn/Fakenham/Melton Constable	1879/1882	1959

Line	Opened	Final Closure
Halesworth to Southwold	1879	1929
Forncett to Wymondham	1881	1939
Melton Constable to Norwich	1882	1959
Denver to Stoke Ferry	1882	1930
Wroxham to County School	1882	1952
Wisbech–Upwell Tramway	1883/1884	1928
Melton Constable to Sheringham*[4]	1884/1887	1964
Cambridge to Mildenhall	1884/1885	1962
Somersham to Ramsey	1889	1930
Woodham Ferrers to Maldon	1889	1939
North Walsham to Cromer	1898	1964
Yarmouth to Lowestoft	1903	1970
Yarmouth Beach to Gorleston	1903	1953
Kelvedon to Tollesbury Pier*[5]	1904	1951
Haughley to Laxfield	1908	1952
Elsenham to Thaxted	1913	1952

*[1]Wells to Walsingham now the Wells & Walsingham Light Railway

*[2]Chappel & Wakes Colne station now the site for the East Anglian Railway Museum

*[3]Stretch near Sible & Castle Hedingham station now Colne Valley Railway

*[4]Holt to Sheringham now the North Norfolk Railway

*[5]Tollesbury to Tollesbury Pier – opened 1907, closed 1921.

†Central Line from 1957

INDEX